THE MADWOMAN OF CHAILLOT

BY JEAN GIRAUDOUX

ADAPTED BY MAURICE VALENCY

★

★

DRAMATISTS
PLAY SERVICE
INC.

THE MADWOMAN OF CHAILLOT was first presented on December 27, 1948, at the Belasco Theatre in New York, by Alfred de Liagre, Jr. The settings and costumes were designed by Christian Berard. The play was directed by Mr. de Liagre with the following cast:

(In the Order of Their Appearance)

THE WAITER	Ralph Smiley
THE LITTLE MAN	Harold Grau
THE PROSPECTOR	Vladimir Sokoloff
THE PRESIDENT	Clarence Derwent
THE BARON	Le Roi Operti
THERESE	Patricia Courtley
THE STREET SINGER	Eugene Cibelli
THE FLOWER GIRL	Millicent Brower
THE RAGPICKER	John Carradine
PAULETTE	Barbara Pond
THE DEAF-MUTE	Martin Kosleck
IRMA	Leora Dana
THE SHOELACE PEDDLER	Maurice Brenner
THE BROKER	Jonathan Harris
THE STREET JUGGLER	John Beahan
DR. JADIN	Sandro Giglio
COUNTESS AURELIA, *The Madwoman of Chaillot*	Martita Hunt
THE DOORMAN	William Chambers
THE POLICEMAN	Ralph Roberts
PIERRE	Alan Shayne
THE SERGEANT	Richard Sanders
THE SEWER-MAN	James Westerfield
MME. CONSTANCE, *The Madwoman of Passy*	Estelle Winwood
MLLE. GABRIELLE, *The Madwoman of St. Sulpice*	Nydia Westman
MME. JOSEPHINE, *The Madwoman of La Concorde*	Doris Rich
THE PRESIDENTS	Clarence Derwent / Jonathan Harris / Le Roi Operti
THE PROSPECTORS	Vladimir Sokoloff / Paul Ryron / Maurice Brenner
THE PRESS AGENTS	Archie Smith / Ralph Roberts / James Westerfield

3

THE LADIES	{	Patricia Courtley
		Barbara Pond
		Sonia Sorel
THE ADOLPHE BERTAUT	{	William Chambers
		Paul Byron
		Gilbert Smith

SCENES

ACT I

The Cafe Terrace of Chez Francis.

ACT II

The Countess' Cellar—21 Rue de Chaillot.

Music for La Belle Mazur (La Belle Polonaise) especially composed by Alexander Haas.

Music for Champagne Mazurka, and incidental music in last scene, especially composed by Albert Hague.

4

THE MADWOMAN OF CHAILLOT

ACT I

SCENE: *The café terrace at* CHEZ FRANCIS, *on the Place de l'Alma in Paris. The Alma is in the stately quarter of Paris known as Chaillot, between the Champs-Elysées and the Seine, across the river from the Eiffel Tower.*

CHEZ FRANCIS *has several rows of tables set out under its awning and, as it is lunch time, a good many of them are occupied.* THE PROSPECTOR *sits at an upstage table taking little sips of water and rolling them over his tongue with the air of a connoisseur.* LITTLE MAN *is sitting at table* U. L. *reading newspaper. Downstage* R., *in front of the tables on the sidewalk is the usual Paris bench, a stout and uncomfortable affair provided by the municipality for the benefit of those who prefer to sit without drinking. The* DOORMAN *crosses* R. *to* L. *and off on bicycle.* STREET SINGER *plays off* R.

TIME: *It is a little before noon in the Spring of next year.*

AT RISE: THERESE, *a blonde, enters* L. *and crosses to table up* R. PRESIDENT *and* BARON *enter behind her to a front table, led by* WAITER.

PRESIDENT. Baron, sit down. This is a historic occasion. It must be properly celebrated. The waiter is going to bring out my special port.

BARON. Splendid.

PRESIDENT. (*Offers his cigar case.*) Cigar?

BARON. Thank you.

PRESIDENT. My private brand. (*They sit at table* L. C.)

BARON. —You know this all gives me the feeling of one of those

5

enchanted mornings in the Arabian Nights when thieves foregather in the market place—thieves—pashas —— (*He sniffs cigar judiciously, and begins lighting it.* STREET SINGER *enters* R.)

PRESIDENT. (*Chuckles.*) Tell me about yourself.

BARON. Well—where shall I begin ——? (STREET SINGER *takes off a battered black felt with a flourish and begins singing an ancient mazurka.*)

STREET SINGER. (*Sings.*)

>   Do you hear, Mademoiselle,
>   Those musicians of hell?

PRESIDENT. Waiter! Get rid of that man.

WAITER. He is singing *La Belle Polonaise.*

PRESIDENT. I didn't ask for the program. I asked you to get rid of him. (WAITER *exits into café.* STREET SINGER *goes by himself* R., *singing.*) As you were saying, Baron ——?

BARON. Well, until I was fifty—(FLOWER GIRL *enters through café door,* C.) my life was relatively uncomplicated. It consisted of selling off one by one the various estates left me by my father. Three years ago I parted with my last farm. Two years ago I lost my last mistress. And now—all that is left me is ——

FLOWER GIRL. (*To* BARON.) Violets, sir?

PRESIDENT. Run along, please. (FLOWER GIRL *moves to* PROSPECTOR, *then exits into café* C.)

BARON. (*Staring after her.*) So that, in short, all I have left now is my name ——

PRESIDENT. Your name is precisely the name we need on our board of directors.

BARON. (*With an inclination of his head.*) Very flattering.

PRESIDENT. You will understand when I tell you that mine has been a very different experience. I came up from the bottom. My mother spent most of her life bent over a washtub in order to send me to school. I'm eternally grateful to her, of course, but I must confess that I no longer remember her face. It was no doubt beautiful—but when I try to recall it, I see only the part she invariably showed me—her rear. (WAITER *brings two glasses.*)

BARON. Very touching —— (POLICE SERGEANT *enters from café, exits* R.)

PRESIDENT. When I was thrown out of school for the fifth and last time, I decided to find out for myself what makes the world go round. I ran errands for an editor, a movie star, a financier ——

I began to understand a little what life is. (WAITER *exits into café*.) Then, one day, in the street, I saw a face —— My rise in life dates from that day.

BARON. Really?

PRESIDENT. One look at that face, and I knew. One look at mine, and he knew. And so I made my first thousand—passing a boxful of counterfeit notes. A year later, I saw another such face. It got me a nice berth in the narcotics business. (RAGPICKER *enters* R.) Since then, all I do is look out for such faces. And now here I am —president of eleven corporations, director of fifty-two companies, and, beginning today, chairman of the board of the international combine in which you have been so good as to accept a post. (RAGPICKER *passes, sees something under* PRESIDENT'S *table, and stoops to pick it up*.) Looking for something?

RAGPICKER. Did you drop this?

PRESIDENT. I never drop anything.

RAGPICKER. Then this hundred-franc note isn't yours?

PRESIDENT. Give it here. (RAGPICKER *gives him note, and goes out* L.)

BARON. Are you sure it's yours?

PRESIDENT. All hundred-franc notes, Baron, are mine.

BARON. Mr. President, there's something I've been wanting to ask you. What exactly is the purpose of our new company?—Or is that an indiscreet question ——?

PRESIDENT. Indiscreet? Not a bit. Merely unusual. As far as I know, you're the first member of a board of directors ever to ask such a question.

BARON. Do we plan to exploit a commodity? A utility ——?

PRESIDENT. My dear sir, I haven't the faintest idea.

BARON. But if you don't know—who does? (BRUNETTE *enters* L., *joins* BLONDE.)

PRESIDENT. Nobody. And at the moment it's becoming just a trifle embarrassing. Yes, my dear Baron, since we are now close business associates, I must confess that for the time being we're in a little trouble.

BARON. I was afraid of that.—The stock issue isn't going well?

PRESIDENT. No, no—on the contrary. The stock issue is going beautifully. Yesterday morning at ten o'clock we offered 500,000 shares to the general public. By 10:05 they were all snapped up at par. By 10:20, when the police finally arrived, our offices were a shambles—you never saw anything so beautiful in your life!

BARON. But in that case—what is the trouble?

PRESIDENT. The trouble is we have a tremendous capital, and not the slightest idea of what to do with it.

BARON. You mean all those people are fighting to buy stock in a company that has no object ——?

PRESIDENT. My dear Baron, do you imagine that when a subscriber buys a share of stock he has any idea of getting behind a counter or digging a ditch? A stock certificate is not a tool, like a shovel, or a commodity, like a pound of cheese. What we sell a customer is not a share in a business, but a view of the Elysian Fields. A financier is a creative artist. Our function is to stimulate the imagination. We are poets!

BARON. But in order to stimulate the imagination, don't you need some field of activity?

PRESIDENT. Not at all. What you need is a name. A name that will stir the pulse, a trumpet call, set the brain awhirl, a movie star, inspire reverence, a cathedral. *United General International Consolidated!* Of course that's been used. That's what a corporation needs.

BARON. And do we have such a name?

PRESIDENT. So far we have only a blank space. In that blank space a name must be printed. Baron, in the course of my life, I have personally organized eleven great corporations on the basis of eleven magnificent names. I have a reputation at stake. This name must be a masterpiece. And if I seem a little nervous today, it's because—somehow—I've racked my brains, but it hasn't come to me.—But somehow, I wish —— Oho! Look at that! Just like the answer to a prayer ——! (BARON *turns and stares in direction of* PROSPECTOR.) You see? There's one. And what a beauty!

BARON. You mean that girl?

PRESIDENT. No, no, not the girl. That face. The one that's drinking water.

BARON. You call that a face? That's a tombstone.

PRESIDENT. It's a milestone. It's a signpost. But is it pointing the way to steel, or wheat, or phosphates?—That's what we have to find out. Ah! He sees me. He understands. He will be over.

BARON. And when he comes ——?

PRESIDENT. He will tell me what to do. (WAITER *enters from café.*)

8

BARON. You mean business is done this way? You mean, you would trust a stranger with a matter of this importance?

PRESIDENT. Baron, I trust neither my wife, nor my daughter, my closest friend, nor my confidential secretary. But a face like that I would trust with my inmost secrets. (DEAF-MUTE *enters* R. BRUNETTE *crosses into café.*) Though we have never laid eyes on each other before, that man and I know each other to the depths of our souls. He's no stranger—he's my brother—he's myself. You'll see. He'll be over in a minute. (DEAF-MUTE *passes slowly among tables, placing a small envelope before each customer. He comes to* PRESIDENT'S *table.*) What is this anyway? A conspiracy? We don't want your envelopes. Take them away. (DEAF-MUTE *makes a short but pointed speech in sign language.*) Waiter, what the devil's he saying?

WAITER. Only Irma understands him.

PRESIDENT. Irma? Who's Irma?

WAITER. (*Calls.*) Irma!—It's the waitress inside, sir.—Irma! (SHOELACE PEDDLER *enters* R. IRMA *comes out. She is twenty. She has the face and figure of an angel.*)

IRMA. Yes?

WAITER. These gentlemen would . . .

PRESIDENT. Tell this fellow to get out of here, for God's sake! (DEAF-MUTE *makes another manual oration.*) What's he trying to say, anyway?

IRMA. (*Down* C.) He says it's an exceptionally beautiful morning, sir ——

PRESIDENT. Who asked him?

IRMA. But, he says, it was nicer before you stuck your face in it.

PRESIDENT. Call the manager! (IRMA *shrugs. She goes back into café.* DEAF-MUTE *walks off* L.)

PEDDLER. Shoelaces? Shoelaces? Post-cards?

BARON. (*Calling* PEDDLER.) I think I could use a shoelace.

PRESIDENT. No, no ——

BARON. (*To* PEDDLER.) Sorry! (PEDDLER *exits* R. BROKER *walks up* L., *and grasps* PRESIDENT'S *hand with enthusiasm.*)

BROKER. Mr. President! My heartiest congratulations! What a day! What a day! (STREET JUGGLER *appears* R. *Removes his coat, folds it carefully, and puts it on bench. Then he opens a suitcase, from which he extracts a number of colored clubs.*)

PRESIDENT. (*Presenting* BROKER.) Baron Tommard of our Board

9

of Directors. My broker. (BROKER *bows. So does* JUGGLER. BROKER *sits down and signals for a drink.* JUGGLER *prepares to juggle.* WAITER *goes into café.*) Well? What news?

BROKER. Listen to this. . . . Ten o'clock this morning. The market opens. (*As he speaks,* JUGGLER *provides a visual counterpart to* BROKER'S *lines, his clubs rising and falling in rhythm to* BROKER'S *words.*) Half million shares issued at par, par value a hundred, quoted on the curb at 124 and we start buying at 126, 127, 129 —and it's going up—up—up—(JUGGLER'S *clubs rise higher and higher.*) 132—133—138—141—141—141—141 ——

BARON. May I ask——?

PRESIDENT. No, no—any explanation would only confuse you —— (*To* BROKER.) Go on ——

BROKER. 10:45 we start selling short on rumors of a Communist plot, market bearish.—141—138—133—132—and it's down— down—down—102—and we start buying back at 93. Eleven o'clock, rumors denied—95—98—101—106—124—141—and by 11:30 we've got it all back—net profit three and a half million francs. (*Sits.*)

PRESIDENT. Classical. Classical. (JUGGLER *bows again. The* LITTLE MAN *leans over from a nearby table, listening intently, and trembling with excitement.*) And how many shares do we reserve to each member of the board?

BROKER. Fifty, as agreed.

PRESIDENT. Bit stingy, don't you think?

BROKER. All right—three thousand.

PRESIDENT. That's a little better. (*To* BARON.) You get the idea?

BARON. I'm beginning to get it.

BROKER. And now we come to the exciting part —— (JUGGLER *prepares to juggle again.*) Listen carefully: with 35% of our funded capital under section 32 I buy fifty thousand United at 36 which I immediately reconvert into 32 thousand National Amalgamated two's preferred which I set up as collateral on 150 thousand General Consols which I deposit against a credit of 15 billion to buy Eastern Hennequin which I immediately turn into Argentine wheat realizing 136% of the original investment which naturally accrues as capital gain and not as corporate income thus saving 12 millions in taxes, and at once convert the 25% cotton reserve into lignite, and as our people swing into action in London and New York, I beat up the price on greige goods from 26 to

10

92—114—203—306—(JUGGLER *by now is juggling his fireballs in the sky.*) 404 —— (LITTLE MAN *can stand no more. Rushes over and dumps a sackful of money on table.*)

LITTLE MAN. Here—take it—please take it!

BROKER. (*Sitting, frigidly.*) Who is this man? What is this money?

LITTLE MAN. It's my life's savings. Every cent. I put it all in your hands.

BROKER. Can't you see we're busy?

LITTLE MAN. But I beg you —— It's my only chance —— Please don't turn me away.

BROKER. Oh, all right. (*He sweeps money into his pocket.*) Well?

LITTLE MAN. I thought—perhaps you'd give me a little re ceipt ——?

PRESIDENT. My dear man, people like us don't give receipts for money. We take them.

LITTLE MAN. Oh, pardon. Of course. I was confused. Here it is. (*Scribbles receipt.*) Thank you—thank you—thank you. (*He rushes off joyfully,* L. STREET SINGER *reappears with* DR. JADIN R. WAITER *brings drink to* BROKER.)

STREET SINGER. (*Sings.*)

> Do you hear, Mademoiselle,
> Those musicians of hell?
>
> (*Music cue No. 1.*[1])

PRESIDENT. What, again? Why does he keep repeating those two lines like a parrot?

WAITER. What can he do if he doesn't know any more and the song's been out of print for years?

BARON. Couldn't he sing a song he knows?

WAITER. He likes this one. He hopes if he keeps singing the beginning someone will turn up who can teach him the end.

PRESIDENT. Tell him to move on. We don't know the song.

DR. JADIN. (*Stops and addresses* PRESIDENT *politely.*) Nor do I, my dear sir. Nor do I. And yet, I'm in exactly the same predicament. I remember just two lines of my favorite song as a child. A mazurka also, in case you're interested ——

PRESIDENT. I'm not.

DR. JADIN. Why is it, I wonder, that one always forgets the words of a mazurka? I suppose they just get lost in that damnable rhythm. All I remember is: (*Sings.*)

11

From England to Spain
I have drunk, it was bliss,
(*Music cue No. 2.*)

STREET SINGER. (*Walks over, and picks up tune.*)
Red wine and champagne
And many a kiss.

DR. JADIN. Oh, God! It all comes back to me —— (*Sings.*)
Red lips and white hands and warm hearts I have known—
Where the nightingales dwell ——

(*Repeats verse. They stroll off together* R. BRUNETTE *enters from café.*)

PRESIDENT. This isn't a café. It's a circus! (PROSPECTOR *gets up slowly and walks toward* PRESIDENT'S *table. Looks down without a word. A tense silence.*)

PROSPECTOR. Well?

PRESIDENT. I need a name.

PROSPECTOR. (*Nods, with complete comprehension.*) I need fifty thousand.

PRESIDENT. Immediately.

PROSPECTOR. Before evening.

PRESIDENT. For a corporation. Something ——

PROSPECTOR. Unusual?

PRESIDENT. Something ——

PROSPECTOR. Provocative?

PRESIDENT. Something ——

PROSPECTOR. Practical.

PRESIDENT. Yes.

PROSPECTOR. Fifty thousand. Cash.

PRESIDENT. (*After exchanging look with* PROSPECTOR.) I'm listening.

PROSPECTOR. *International Substrate of Paris, Inc.*

PRESIDENT. (*Snaps his fingers.*) That's it! (*To* BROKER.) Pay him off. (BROKER *pays with* LITTLE MAN'S *money.*) Now—what does it mean?

PROSPECTOR. It means what it says. I'm a prospector.

PRESIDENT. (*Rises.*) A prospector! Allow me to shake your hand. —Baron. You are in the presence of one of nature's noblemen. Shake his hand.—This is Baron Tommard.

(*They shake hands.*) It is this man, my dear Baron, who smells out in the bowels of the earth those deposits of metal or liquid

12

on which can be founded the only social unit of which our age is capable—the corporation. Sit down, please. (*They all sit.* PROSPECTOR *between* PRESIDENT *and* BARON.) And now that we have a name ——

PROSPECTOR. You need a property.

PRESIDENT. Precisely.

PROSPECTOR. I have one.

PRESIDENT. A claim?

PROSPECTOR. Terrific.

PRESIDENT. Foreign?

PROSPECTOR. French.

BARON. In Indo-China?

BROKER. Morocco?

PRESIDENT. In France?

PROSPECTOR. (*Matter-of-fact.*) In Paris.

PRESIDENT. In Paris? You've been prospecting in Paris?

BARON. For women, no doubt.

PRESIDENT. For art?

BROKER. For gold?

PROSPECTOR. Oil.

BROKER. He's crazy.

PRESIDENT. Sh —— He's inspired.

PROSPECTOR. You think I'm crazy. Well, they thought Columbus was crazy.

BARON. Oil in Paris?

BROKER. But how is it possible?

PROSPECTOR. It's not only possible. It's certain.

PRESIDENT. Tell us.

PROSPECTOR. You don't know, my dear sir, what treasures Paris conceals. Paris is the least prospected place in the world. We've gone over the rest of the planet with a fine-tooth comb. But has anyone ever thought of looking for oil in Paris? Nobody. Before me, that is.

PRESIDENT. Genius!

PROSPECTOR. No. Just a practical man. I use my head.

BARON. But why has nobody ever thought of this before?

PROSPECTOR. The treasures of the earth, my dear sir, are not easy to find nor to get at. They are invariably guarded by dragons. Doubtless there is some reason for this. For once we've dug out and consumed the internal ballast of the planet, the chances are it will shoot off on some irresponsible tangent and smash itself up in the sky. Well, that's the risk we take. Anyway, that's not my business. A prospector has enough to worry about.

BARON. I know—snakes—tarantulas—fleas ——

PROSPECTOR. Worse than that, sir. Civilization.

PRESIDENT. Does that annoy you?

PROSPECTOR. Civilization gets in our way all the time. In the first place, it covers the earth with cities and towns which are damned awkward to dig up when you want to see what's underneath. It's not only the real-estate people—you can always do business with them—it's human sentimentality. How do you do business with that?

PRESIDENT. I see what you mean.

PROSPECTOR. They say that where we pass, nothing ever grows again. What of it? Is a park any better than a coal mine? What's a mountain got that a slag pile hasn't? What would you rather have in your garden—an almond tree or an oil well?

PRESIDENT. Well ——

PROSPECTOR. Exactly. But what's the use of arguing with these fools? Imagine the choicest place you ever saw for an excavation, and what do they put there? A playground for children! Civilization!

PRESIDENT. Just show us the point where you want to start digging. We'll do the rest. Even if it's in the middle of the Louvre. Where's the oil?

PROSPECTOR. Perhaps you think it's easy to make an accurate fix in an area like Paris where everything conspires to put you off the scent? Women—perfume—flowers—history. You can talk all you like about geology, but an oil deposit, gentlemen, has to be smelled out. I have a good nose. I go further. I have a phenomenal nose. But the minute I get the right whiff—the minute I'm on the scent—a fragrance rises from what I take to be the spiritual deposits of the past—and I'm completely at sea. Now take this very point, for example, this very spot.

BARON. You mean—right here in Chaillot?

PROSPECTOR. Right under here.

PRESIDENT. Good heavens! (*Looks under his chair.*)

PROSPECTOR. It's taken me months to locate this spot.

BARON. But what in the world makes you think ——?

PROSPECTOR. Do you know this place, Baron?

14

BARON. Well, I've been sitting here for thirty years.

PROSPECTOR. Did you ever taste the water?

BARON. The water? Good God, no.

PROSPECTOR. It is plain to see that you are no prospector. A prospector, Baron, is addicted to water as a drunkard to wine. Water, gentlemen, is the one substance from which the earth can conceal nothing. It sucks out its innermost secrets and brings them to our very lips. Well—beginning at Notre Dame, where I first caught the scent of oil three months ago, I worked my way across Paris, glassful by glassful, sampling the water, until at last I came to this café. And here—just two days ago—I took a sip. My heart began to thump. Was it possible that I was deceived? I took another, a third, a fourth, a fifth. I was trembling like a leaf. But there was no mistake. I had found it. And each time that I drank, my taste-buds thrilled to the most exquisite flavor known to a prospector—the flavor of—(*With utmost lyricism.*) petroleum!

PRESIDENT. Waiter! Some water and four glasses. Hurry. This round, gentlemen, is on me. And—I shall propose as a toast— International Substrate of Paris, Incorporated. (WAITER *brings a decanter and glasses.* PRESIDENT *pours out water amid profound silence. Toast routine. They taste it with the air of connoisseurs savoring something that has never before passed human lips. Then they look at each other doubtfully.* PROSPECTOR *pours himself a second glass and drinks it off.*) Well ——

BROKER. Yes ——

PROSPECTOR. Get it?

BARON. Tastes queer.

PROSPECTOR. That's it. To the unpractised palate it tastes queer. But to the taste-buds of the expert—ah!

BARON. Still, there's one thing I don't quite understand ——

PROSPECTOR. Yes?

BARON. This café doesn't have its own well, does it?

PROSPECTOR. Of course not. This is Paris water.

BROKER. Then why should it taste different here than anywhere else?

PROSPECTOR. Because, my dear sir, the pipes that carry this water pass deep through the earth, and the earth just here is soaked with oil, and this oil permeates the pores of the iron and flavors the water it carries. Ever so little, yes—but quite enough to betray its presence to the sensitive tongue of the specialist.

BARON. I see.

PROSPECTOR. I don't say that everyone is capable of tasting it. No. But I—I can detect the presence of oil in water that has passed within fifteen miles of a deposit. Under special circumstances, twenty.

PRESIDENT. Phenomenal!

PROSPECTOR. And so here I am with the greatest discovery of the age on my hands—but the blasted authorities won't let me drill a single well unless I show them the oil! Now how the hell can I show them the oil unless they let me dig? Completely baffled! Eh?

PRESIDENT. What? A man like you?

PROSPECTOR. That's what they think. That's what they want. Have you noticed this extraordinary convocation of vagabonds buzzing (DOORMAN *enters* R., *crosses into café* C.) about protectively like bees around a hive? Do you know why it is? Because they know! They're all in league together—it's a plot to distract us, to turn us from our purpose. (WAITER *enters from café.*) Well, let them try. I know there's oil here. And I'm going to dig it up, if necessary, even if I —— (*He smiles.*) Shall I tell you my little plan?

PRESIDENT. By all means.

PROSPECTOR. Well —— For heaven's sake, what's that? (*At this point, the* MADWOMAN [COUNTESS] *enters* R. *She is dressed in the grand fashion of 1885, a taffeta skirt with an immense train—which she has gathered up by means of a clothespin—ancient button shoes, and a hat in the style of Marie Antoinette. She wears a lorgnette on a chain, and an enormous cameo pin at her throat. In her hand she carries a small basket. She walks in with great dignity, extracts a dinner bell from the bosom of her dress, and rings it sharply.* IRMA *appears from café.*)

COUNTESS. Are my bones ready, Irma?

IRMA. There won't be much today, Countess. We had broilers. Can you wait while the gentleman inside finishes eating?

COUNTESS. And my gizzard.

IRMA. I'll try to get it away from him.

COUNTESS. If he eats my gizzard, save me the giblets. They will do for the tomcat that lives under the bridge. He likes a few giblets now and again.

IRMA. Yes, Countess. (IRMA *goes back into café.* COUNTESS *takes a few steps and stops in front of* PRESIDENT'S *table. She examines him with undisguised disapproval.*)

PRESIDENT. Waiter! Ask that woman to move on.

WAITER. Sorry, sir. This is her café.

PRESIDENT. She's the manager of the café?

WAITER. She's the Madwoman of Chaillot.

PRESIDENT. A madwoman? She's mad?

WAITER. Who says she's mad?

PRESIDENT. You just said so yourself, stupid.

WAITER. Look, sir. You asked me who she was. And I told you. What's mad about her? She's the Madwoman of Chaillot.

PRESIDENT. Call a policeman. (COUNTESS *whistles through her fingers. At once,* DOORMAN *runs out of café. He has three scarves in his hands.*)

DOORMAN. Yes, Countess?

COUNTESS. Have you found it? My feather boa?

DOORMAN. Not yet, Countess. Three scarves. But no boa.

COUNTESS. It's five years since I lost it. Surely you've had time to find it?

DOORMAN. Take one of these, Countess. Nobody's claimed them.

COUNTESS. A boa like that doesn't vanish, you know. A feather boa nine feet long!

DOORMAN. How about this yellow one?

COUNTESS. With my pink rose and my green veil? You're joking! Let me see the blue one. (*She tries it on.*) How does it look?

DOORMAN. (*Exits* R.) Terrific. (*With a magnificent gesture, she flings scarf about her, upsetting* PRESIDENT'S *glass and drenching his trousers with water. She stalks, without a glance at him, to garden table* L. *and sits.*)

PRESIDENT. (*Rising.*) Waiter! I'm making a complaint.

WAITER. Against whom?

PRESIDENT. Against her! Against you! The whole gang of you! That singer! That shoelace peddler! That female lunatic! Or whatever you call her!

BARON. Calm yourself, Mr. President —— (WAITER *goes into café.*)

PRESIDENT. I'll do nothing of the sort! Baron, the first thing we have to do is to get rid of these people! Good heavens, look at them! Every size, shape, color and period of history imaginable. It's utter anarchy! I tell you, sir, the only safeguard of order and discipline in the modern world is a standardized worker with interchangeable parts. (*Sits.*) Here, the manager —— And there

17

—one composite drudge grunting and sweating all over the world. Just we two.—Ah, how beautiful! How easy on the eyes! How restful for the conscience!

BARON. Yes, yes, of course —— (*Enter* FLOWER GIRL, WAITER *from café.* SERGEANT *from* L. *to* MADWOMAN.)

PRESIDENT. Order. Symmetry. Balance. But instead of that, what? Here in Chaillot, the very citadel of management, these insolent phantoms of the past come to beard us with their raffish individualism—with the right of the voiceless to sing, of the dumb to make speeches, of trousers to have no seats and bosoms to have dinner bells!

BARON. But, after all, do these people matter?

PRESIDENT. My dear sir, wherever the poor are happy, and the servants proud, and the mad are respected, our power is at an end. Look at that! That waiter! That madwoman! That flower girl! Do I get that sort of service? And suppose that I—president of twelve corporations and ten times a millionaire—were to stick a gladiolus in my buttonhole and start yelling—(*He rises and yells.*) Are my bones ready, Irma? (*Exit* FLOWER GIRL *into café.* SERGEANT *exits* L.)

BARON. (*Reprovingly.*) Mr. President —— (PEOPLE *at the adjoining tables turn and stare with raised eyebrows.* WAITER *starts to come over.*)

PRESIDENT. You see?—Now.

PROSPECTOR. We were discussing my plan.

PRESIDENT. Ah, yes, your plan. (*He glances in direction of* MADWOMAN'S *table.*) Careful—she's looking at us.

PROSPECTOR. Do you know what a bomb is?

PRESIDENT. I'm told they explode.

PROSPECTOR. Exactly. You see that white building across the river. Do you happen to know what that is?

PRESIDENT. I do not.

PROSPECTOR. It's the office of the City Architect. That man has stubbornly refused to give me a permit to drill for oil anywhere within the limits of the city of Paris. I've tried everything with him—influence, bribes, threats. He says I'm crazy. But now ——
(DR. JADIN *re-enters* R. *and doffs his hat politely. He is somewhat ostentatiously respectable — gloved, pomaded, and carefully dressed, with a white handkerchief peeping out of his breast pocket.*)

18

PRESIDENT. Oh, my God! Now what's he trying to sell us?

DR. JADIN. Nothing but health, sir. Or rather the health of the feet. But, remember—as the foot goes, so goes the man. May I present myself ——? Dr. Gaspard Jadin, French Navy, retired. Former specialist in the extraction of ticks and chiggers. At present specializing in the extraction of bunions and corns. In case of sudden emergency, Martial the waiter will furnish my home address. My office is here, second row, second table, week days, twelve to five. Thank you very much. (*Moves upstage.*) How are your gallstones today, Martial?

WAITER. Fine. Fine. They rattle like anything.

DR. JADIN. Splendid. (*He spies* COUNTESS.) Good morning, Countess. How's the floating kidney? Still afloat? (*She nods graciously.*) Splendid. Splendid. So long as it floats, it can't sink. (*He sits at his table, L.*)

PRESIDENT. Gentlemen, this is impossible! Let's go somewhere else.

PROSPECTOR. No, no—it must be nearly noon.

PRESIDENT. It's five to twelve.

PROSPECTOR. In five minutes' time you're going to see that City Architect blown up, building and all—boom!

BROKER. Are you serious?

PROSPECTOR. That imbecile has no one to blame but himself. Yesterday noon he got my ultimatum—he's had twenty-four hours to think it over. No permit? All right. I'm sorry. Within two minutes my agent is going to drop a little package in his coal bin. And three minutes after that, precisely at noon ——

BROKER. (*Gestures.*) Voom!

BARON. You prospectors certainly use modern methods.

PROSPECTOR. The method may be modern. But the idea is old. To get at the treasure, it has always been necessary to slay the dragon that guards it. I guarantee that after this, the City Architect will be more reasonable. The new one, I mean.

PRESIDENT. Don't you think we're sitting a little close for comfort?

PROSPECTOR. Oh, no, no. Don't worry. And, above all, don't stare. We may be watched. (*Chime strikes noon—ad lib. off* R.) Why, that's noon. Something's wrong! Good God! What's this? (*Preceded by* DEAF-MUTE, *a* POLICEMAN *staggers in, bearing a lifeless body* [PIERRE] *on his shoulders in the manner prescribed as " The Fireman's Lift." He places body on bench* R. BLONDE *rises.*) It's Pierre! My agent! (*Rises, crosses to him* D. R.) I say, Officer,

what's that you've got? (WAITER *moves down.*)

POLICEMAN. Drowned man.

WAITER. (*Crosses to bench.*) He's not drowned. His clothes are dry. He's been slugged.

POLICEMAN. Slugged is also correct. He was just jumping off the bridge when I came along and pulled him back. I slugged him, naturally, so he wouldn't drag me under. Life Saving Manual, Rule 5: " In cases where there is danger of being dragged under, it is necessary to render the subject unconscious by means of a sharp blow." He's had that. (*He loosens clothes and begins applying artificial respiration.*)

PROSPECTOR. The stupid idiot! That's what comes of employing amateurs! But what the devil did he do with the bomb?

PRESIDENT. You don't think he'll give you away?

PROSPECTOR. Don't worry. (*He walks over to* POLICEMAN.) Say, what do you think you're doing?

POLICEMAN. Lifesaving. Artificial respiration. First aid to the drowning.

PROSPECTOR. But he's not drowning.

POLICEMAN. But he thinks he is.

PROSPECTOR. You'll never bring him round that way, my friend. That is meant for people who drown in water. It's no good at all for those who drown without water.

POLICEMAN. What am I supposed to do? I've just been sworn in. It's my first day on the beat. I can't afford to get in trouble. I've got to go by the book.

PROSPECTOR. (PRESIDENT *rises, crosses to* L. *of* PROSPECTOR.) Perfectly simple. Take him back to the bridge where you found him and throw him in. Then you can save his life and you'll get a medal. This way, you'll only get fined for slugging an innocent man.

POLICEMAN. What do you mean, innocent? He was just going to jump when I grabbed him.

PROSPECTOR. Have you any proof of that?

POLICEMAN. Well, I saw him.

PROSPECTOR. Written proof? Witnesses?

POLICEMAN. No, but——

PROSPECTOR. Then don't waste time arguing. You're in trouble. Quick—before anybody notices—throw him in and dive after him. It's the only way out.

POLICEMAN. But I don't swim.

PRESIDENT. You'll learn how on the way down. Before you were born, did you know how to breathe?

POLICEMAN. (*Convinced.*) All right.—Here we go. (*He starts lifting body.* COUNTESS *rises and moves* R. C.)

DR. JADIN. (*Crossing down to* R. *of* PROSPECTOR.) One moment, please, one moment. I don't like to interfere, but it's my professional duty to point out that medical science has definitely established the fact of intra-uterine respiration. Consequently, this policeman, even before he was born, knew not only how to breathe but how to cough, hiccup and belch.

PRESIDENT. Suppose he did—how does it concern you?

DR. JADIN. On the other hand, medical science has never established the fact of intra-uterine swimming or diving. Under the circumstances we are forced to the opinion, Officer, that if you dive in you will probably drown.

POLICEMAN. You think so?

PROSPECTOR. And who asked you for an opinion?

PRESIDENT. Pay no attention to that quack, Officer.

DR. JADIN. Quack, sir?

PROSPECTOR. See here. This is not a medical matter. It's a legal problem. The officer has made a grave error. He's new. We're trying to help him.

BROKER. He's probably afraid of the water.

POLICEMAN. Nothing of the sort. Officially I'm afraid of nothing. But I always follow doctor's orders.

DR. JADIN. You see, Officer, when a child is born ——

PROSPECTOR. Now, what does he care about when a child is born? He's got a dying man on his hands —— Officer, if you want my advice ——

POLICEMAN. It so happens, I care a lot about when a child is born. It's part of my duty to aid and assist any woman in childbirth or labor.

PRESIDENT. Can you imagine! Prospector —— (BARON, BROKER, PROSPECTOR, PRESIDENT *huddle* C.)

POLICEMAN. (*Up to* D. R.) Is it true, Doctor, what they say, that when you have twins, the first born is the youngest?

DR. JADIN. Oh, quite correct.

POLICEMAN. God! The things a policeman is supposed to know!

21

Doctor, what does it means if, when I get up in the morning sometimes —— (*He turns upstage.*)

PROSPECTOR. (*Nudging* PRESIDENT *meaningfully.*) The old woman ——

BROKER. Come on, Baron.

PRESIDENT. I think we'd better all run along.

PROSPECTOR. Leave him to me.

PRESIDENT. I'll see you later. (PRESIDENT *steals off* L. *with* BARON *and* BROKER.)

POLICEMAN. (*Still in conference with* DR. JADIN.) —Don't you think it's a bit risky for a man to marry after forty-five? (BROKER *runs in breathlessly.*)

BROKER. Officer! Officer! (IRMA *enters from café with* WAITER, *who places pillow under* PIERRE'S *head.* DEAF-MUTE *off* R. GIRLS *gather their things from table.*)

POLICEMAN. What's the trouble?

BROKER. Quick! Two women are calling for help—on the sidewalk—Avenue Wilson!

POLICEMAN. Two women at once? Standing up or lying down?

BROKER. You'd better go and see. Quick!

PROSPECTOR. You better take the doctor with you.

POLICEMAN. Come along, Doctor, come along —— (*He starts out* L., DOCTOR *following.* POLICEMAN *points back to* PIERRE.) Oh, tell him to wait till I get back. (PROSPECTOR *moves over toward* PIERRE, *but* IRMA *crosses in front of him, and takes* PIERRE'S *hand.*)

IRMA. (*Sitting on bench.*) How beautiful he is! Is he dead, Martial?

WAITER. (*Handing her a pocket mirror.*) Hold this mirror to his mouth. If it clouds over ——

IRMA. It clouds over.

WAITER. He's alive. (*Holds out his hand for the mirror.*)

IRMA. Just a sec —— (*She rubs it clean and looks at herself intently. Before handing it back, she fixes her hair and applies her lipstick.*) Oh, look—he's opened his eyes! (PIERRE *opens his eyes, stares intently at* IRMA, *murmurs:* "*How beautiful!*" *and closes them again with the expression of a man who is among the angels.*)

VOICE. (*From within café.*) Irma!

IRMA. Coming. (*Rises.*) Coming. (*Runs off into café.* PROSPECTOR *moves toward* PIERRE *again, but the* COUNTESS'S *eagle eye stops*

22

bim. He shrugs and exits L. *with* BROKER. WAITER *exits into café.* COUNTESS *at once takes her place on bench, and* PIERRE'S *hand.* PIERRE *sits up suddenly, and finds himself staring not at* IRMA, *but into the very peculiar face of* COUNTESS. *His expression changes.)*

COUNTESS. You're looking at my iris. Isn't it beautiful?

PIERRE. Very. *(He drops back, exhausted.)*

COUNTESS. The sergeant was good enough to say it becomes me. But I had to tell him quite frankly that I no longer trust his taste. Yesterday the flower girl gave me a lily, and he said it didn't suit me.

PIERRE. *(Weakly.)* It's beautiful.

COUNTESS. He'll be very happy to know that you agree with him. He's really quite sensitive. *(She calls.)* Sergeant!

PIERRE. No, please—don't call the police.

COUNTESS. But I must—I think I hurt his feelings.

PIERRE. Let me go, Madame.

COUNTESS. No, no. Stay where you are. Sergeant! *(PIERRE struggles weakly to get up.)*

PIERRE. Please let me go.

COUNTESS. I'll do nothing of the sort. When you let someone go, you never see him again. I let Charlotte Mazumet go. I never saw her again.

PIERRE. Oh, my head!

COUNTESS. I let Adolphe Bertaut go. And I never saw him again.

PIERRE. Oh, God!

COUNTESS. Except once. Thirty years later. In the market. He had changed a great deal—he didn't know me. He sneaked a melon from right under my nose, the only good one of the year.—Ah, here we are. Sergeant! *(POLICE SERGEANT comes in, with importance, crossing from* L.)

SERGEANT. I'm in a hurry, Countess.

COUNTESS. With regard to the iris. This young man agrees with you. He says it suits me.

SERGEANT. *(Going.)* There's a man drowning in the Seine.

COUNTESS. He's not. He's drowning here. You needn't hurry. Because I'm holding him tight—as I should have held Adolphe Bertaut. But if I let him go, I'm sure he will go and drown in the Seine. He's a lot better looking than Adolphe Bertaut, wouldn't you say? *(PIERRE sighs deeply.)*

SERGEANT. How would I know?

23

COUNTESS. I've shown you his photograph.—The one with the bicycle.

SERGEANT. Oh, yes.—The one with the hare-lip.

COUNTESS. I've told you a hundred times! Adolphe Bertaut had no harelip. That was a scratch in the negative. (SERGEANT *takes out notebook and pencil.*) What are you doing?

SERGEANT. I am taking down the drowned man's name, given name and date of birth.

COUNTESS. You think that's going to stop him from jumping in the river? To tell him the date of his birth?

SERGEANT. I'm not going to tell him. He's going to tell me.

COUNTESS. I wouldn't tell you mine. Don't be silly, Sergeant. Put that book away and console him.

SERGEANT. Console him?

COUNTESS. When people want to die, it is your job to speak out in praise of life. Not mine.

SERGEANT. I should speak out in praise of life?

COUNTESS. I assume you have some motive for interfering with people's attempts to kill each other, and rob each other, and run each other over? If you believe that life has some value, tell him so. As a guardian of the state, surely you must have some idea of the value of life?

SERGEANT. You're right, Countess —— Now look, young fellow ——

COUNTESS. His name is Roderick.

PIERRE. My name is not Roderick.

COUNTESS. Yes, it is. It's noon. At noon all men are called Roderick.

SERGEANT. Except Adolphe Bertaut.

COUNTESS. In the days of Adolphe Bertaut, we had to change the men, when we got tired of their names. Nowadays, we're more practical—each hour on the hour all names are automatically changed. The men remain the same. But you're not here to discuss Adolphe Bertaut, Sergeant. You're here to convince the young man that life is worth living.

PIERRE. It isn't.

SERGEANT. Quiet. Now then—what was the idea of jumping off the bridge, anyway?

COUNTESS. The idea was to land in the river. Roderick doesn't seem to be at all confused about that.

24

SERGEANT. Now how can I convince anybody that life is worth living if you keep interrupting all the time?

COUNTESS. I'll be quiet.

SERGEANT. First of all, Mr. Roderick, you have to realize that suicide is a crime against the state. And why is it a crime against the state? Because every time anybody commits suicide, that means one soldier less for the army, one taxpayer less for the ——

COUNTESS. Sergeant—are you a lover of life—or a tax collector?

SERGEANT. A lover of life?

COUNTESS. Well, surely, in all these years, you must have found something worth living for. Some secret pleasure, or passion. Tell him what it is. Don't blush.

SERGEANT. Who's blushing? Well, naturally, yes—I have my passions—like everybody else. The fact is, since you ask me—I love —to play—casino. And if the gentleman would like to join me, by and by when I go off duty, we can sit down to a nice little game in the back room with a nice cold glass of beer. If he wants to kill an hour, that is.

COUNTESS. He doesn't want to kill an hour. He wants to kill himself. I defy anybody to stop dying on your account.

SERGEANT. Go ahead, if you can do any better.

COUNTESS. Oh, this is not a difficult case at all. In the first place, why should he want to die when he's just this minute fallen in love with someone who has fallen in love with him?

PIERRE. She hasn't. How could she?

COUNTESS. Oh, yes, she has. She was holding your hand, just as I'm holding it now, when all of a sudden —— Did you ever know Marshal Canrobert's niece?

SERGEANT. How could he know Marshal Canrobert's niece?

COUNTESS. Lots of people knew her—when she was alive. (PIERRE *begins to struggle energetically.*) No, no, Roderick—stop—stop!

SERGEANT. You see—you won't do any better than I did.

COUNTESS. No? Let's bet. My iris against one of your gold buttons? Right?

SERGEANT. Right.

COUNTESS. Roderick, I know very well why you were in such a hurry to drown yourself.

PIERRE. You don't at all.

COUNTESS. It's because that prospector wanted you to commit a horrible crime. (WAITER *enters from café with beer for* SERGEANT, *who sits table* C.)

PIERRE. How do you know that?

COUNTESS. He stole my boa, and now he wants you to kill me.

PIERRE. Well, not exactly.

COUNTESS. It wouldn't be the first time they've tried it. But I'm not so easy to get rid of, my boy, oh, no —— Because —— (DOORMAN *comes in on his bicycle—ringing bell—crosses* L. *to* R. *and off*.)

DOORMAN. Take it easy, Sergeant.

SERGEANT. I'm busy saving a drowning man.

COUNTESS. —They can't kill me because—I have no desire to die.

PIERRE. You're fortunate.

COUNTESS. To be alive is to be fortunate, Roderick.—Of course, in the morning, when you first awake, it doesn't always seem so very gay. When you take your hair out of the drawer, and your teeth out of the glass, you are quite likely to feel a little out of place in this naughty world. Particularly if you've just been dreaming that you're a little girl on a pony looking for strawberries in the woods. But all you need in order to feel the call of life again is a letter in the mail giving you your schedule for the day. You write it to yourself the day before—that's the safest. (WAITER *and* SERGEANT *move down to bench.*) Here are my assignments for this morning: to mend my petticoats with red thread, to curl my ostrich feathers, to write my grandmother, etcetera, etcetera. And when I've washed my face with rosewater, and powdered it, not with this awful ricepowder they sell nowadays, which does nothing for the skin—but with a cake of pure white starch—and put on my pins, rings, brooches, pearls, bracelets and earrings—in short, when I am dressed for my coffee, and have had a good look at myself, not in the glass, naturally—it lies—but in the side of the brass gong that once belonged to Admiral Courbet—then, Roderick, then I'm armed, I'm strong, I'm ready to begin again. (PIERRE *is listening now intently, tears in his eyes.*)

PIERRE. Oh, Madame ——! Oh, Madame ——!

COUNTESS. After that everything is pure delight. First the morning paper. Not, of course, these current sheets full of lies and vulgarity. I always read the *Gaulois*, the issue of March 22, 1903 —it's by far the best. It has some delightful scandal, some excellent fashion notes, and, of course, the last minute bulletin on the death of Léonide Leblanc. She used to live next door, poor woman, and when I learn of her death every morning, it gives me quite a shock. I'd gladly lend you my copy, but it's in tatters.

SERGEANT. Couldn't we find him a copy in some library, maybe?

COUNTESS. I doubt it.

PIERRE. Go on, Madame. Go on!

COUNTESS. And so, when you've taken your fruit salts—not in water, naturally—for no matter what they say, it's water that gives you gas—but with a bit of spiced cake—(DEAF-MUTE *enters* L., *crosses to* SERGEANT.) and put on your rings, earrings, brooches and pearls—then, Roderick, then in sunlight or rain, Chaillot calls and it is time to dress for your morning walk. This takes much longer, of course—without a maid, impossible to do it under an hour, what with your corset, corset-cover and drawers, all of which lace or button in the back. I asked Madame Lanvin a while ago to fit the drawers with zippers. She was quite charming, but she declined. She thought it would spoil the style.

WAITER. I know a place where they put zippers on anything.

COUNTESS. I think Lanvin knows best.—But I really manage quite well. What I do now is, I lace them up in front, then twist them around to the back. It's quite simple, really. Then you choose a lorgnette, and then comes the usual fruitless search for the feather boa that your prospector stole—I know it was he: he didn't dare look me in the eye—(*Enter* RAGPICKER *from* L. *Crosses to* L. C.) and then all you need is a rubber band to slip around your parasol —I lost the catch the day I struck the cat that was stalking the pigeon—it was worth it. I earned my wages that day!

RAGPICKER. Countess, if you can use it, I found a nice umbrella catch the other day with a cat's eye in it.

COUNTESS. No, thank you, Ragpicker. They say these eyes sometimes come to life and fill with tears. I'd be afraid ——

PIERRE. Go on, Madame, go on ——

COUNTESS. Ah! So life's beginning to interest you, is it? You see how beautiful it is?

PIERRE. Oh, what a fool I've been!

COUNTESS. Then, Roderick, I begin my rounds. I have my cats to feed, my dogs to pet, my plants to water. I have to see what the evil ones are up to in the district—those who hate animals, those who hate flowers, those who hate people. I watch them sneaking off in the morning to put on their disguises—to the baths, to the beauty parlors, to the barbers. But when they come out again with blond hair and false whiskers, to pull up my flowers and poison my dogs, they can't fool me. I'm there, and I'm ready. All you have to do to break their power is to cut across their path from the left. That isn't always easy. Vice moves swiftly. But I have a good long stride and I generally manage —— Don't I, my friends? (*General agreement.*) Yes—the flowers have been marvellous this year. And the butcher's dog on the Rue Bizet, in spite of that wretch who tried to poison him, is friskier than ever ——

SERGEANT. That dog had better watch out. He has no license.

COUNTESS. He doesn't seem to feel the need for one.

RAGPICKER. The Duchess de la Rochefoucauld's whippet is getting awfully thin ——

COUNTESS. What can I do? She bought that dog full grown from a kennel where they didn't know his right name. A dog without his right name is bound to get thin.

RAGPICKER. I've got a friend who knows a lot about dogs—an Arab ——

COUNTESS. Ask him to call on the Duchess. She receives Thursdays five to seven.—You see, Roderick, that's life. How does it seem to you now?

PIERRE. It seems marvellous.

COUNTESS. Sergeant. My button. (*With a salute* SERGEANT *gives her a button and exits* R.) That's only the morning! Wait till I tell you about the afternoon. In the —— (*At this point* PROSPECTOR *enters* L.)

PROSPECTOR. (*Crossing to* C.) All right, Pierre. Come along with me.

PIERRE. I'm perfectly all right here.

PROSPECTOR. I said, come along now.

PIERRE. (*To* COUNTESS.) I'd better go, Madame.

COUNTESS. No!

PIERRE. It's no use. Please let go my hand!

COUNTESS. Stay where you are. I'm holding your hand because I shall need your arm in a few minutes to take me home. I'm very easily frightened.

PROSPECTOR. Madame, will you oblige me by letting my friend go?

COUNTESS. (*Rising.*) I will not oblige you in any way.

PROSPECTOR. All right. Then I'll oblige you ——! (*She hits him over back with her parasol.*)

PIERRE. Countess ——

PROSPECTOR. (*Calling.*) Officer, officer! (COUNTESS *whistles.* DOOR-MAN *comes in from* L., *then* STREET SINGER, JUGGLER *and* FLOWER GIRL *and* IRMA *come in* R. *and from café. Lastly* SERGEANT.)

SERGEANT. What's the trouble here?

PROSPECTOR. Officer! Arrest this woman! She refuses to let this man go.

SERGEANT. Why should she?

PROSPECTOR. It's against the law for a woman to detain a man on the street.

IRMA. Suppose it's her son whom she's found again after twenty years?

RAGPICKER. (*Gallantly.*) Or her long lost brother? The Countess is not so old!

COUNTESS. Thank you, Ragpicker, thank you.

PROSPECTOR. Officer—this is a clear case of disorderly conduct. (DEAF-MUTE *interrupts with frantic signals.*)

COUNTESS. Irma, what's the Deaf-Mute saying?

IRMA. He says the young man is in danger of his life. He mustn't go with him.

PROSPECTOR. What does he know?

IRMA. He knows everything.

PROSPECTOR. Officer, I'll have to take your number.

COUNTESS. Take his number. It's 2133. It adds up to nine. It will bring you luck.

SERGEANT. Countess, between ourselves, what are you holding him for, anyway?

COUNTESS. I'm holding him because I want to hold him. He's the first man I've ever really held, and I'm enjoying it. And I'm holding him because as long as I hold him he's free.

PROSPECTOR. Pierre—I'm giving you fair warning . . .

COUNTESS. And I'm holding him because Irma wants me to hold him. If I let him go, it will break her heart.

IRMA. Oh, Countess! (PIERRE *sits back.*)

SERGEANT. (*Pushing* PROSPECTOR L.) All right, you. You're blocking traffic.

PROSPECTOR. (*Menacingly.*) I have your number.

SERGEANT. Nobody's holding you. Move on.

PROSPECTOR. (*To* PIERRE.) You'll regret it, Pierre. (*Exit* PROS-PECTOR L. SERGEANT, DEAF-MUTE, DOORMAN *block him so he must exit.*)

29

PIERRE. Thank you, Countess. (RAGPICKER *sits table down* L. DEAF-MUTE *stands* L. *of him.* DOORMAN *sits on table upstage of* RAGPICKER. JUGGLER, STREET SINGER *down* R. PEDDLER, FLOWER GIRL, IRMA *upstage of bench.*)

COUNTESS. (*Moving to* C.) They're blackmailing you, are they? (PIERRE *nods.*) What did you do? Murder someone?

PIERRE. Oh, no.

COUNTESS. Steal something?

PIERRE. No.

COUNTESS. What then?

PIERRE. I forged a signature.

COUNTESS. Whose signature?

PIERRE. My father's. To a note.

COUNTESS. And this man has the paper, I suppose?

PIERRE. He promised to tear it up, if I did what he wanted. But I couldn't do it.

COUNTESS. (*Sitting on bench,* L. *of* PIERRE.) But the man is mad! Does he really want to destroy the whole of Chaillot? (SERGEANT *sits table* u. C.)

PIERRE. He wants to destroy the whole city.

COUNTESS. (*Laughs.*) Fantastic.

PIERRE. It's not funny, Countess. He can do it. He's mad, but he's powerful, and he has friends. Their machines are already drawn up and waiting. In three months' time you may see Paris covered by a forest of derricks and drills.

COUNTESS. But what are they looking for? Have they lost something?

PIERRE. They're looking for oil, Countess. They're convinced that Paris is sitting on a lake of oil.

COUNTESS. Suppose it is? What harm does it do? (DOORMAN *sits table* L. C. *up.*)

PIERRE. They want to bring the oil up to the surface, Countess.

COUNTESS. I never heard of anything so silly! Is that a reason to destroy a city? What do they want with this oil?

PIERRE. They want to make war, Countess.

COUNTESS. Oh, dear, let's forget about these horrible men. The world is beautiful. It's happy. That's how God made it. No man can change it.

WAITER. (*Upstage of bench.*) Ah, Countess, if you only knew ——

30

COUNTESS. If I only knew what?

WAITER. Shall we tell her now?

COUNTESS. What is it you are hiding from me?

RAGPICKER. Nothing, Countess. It's you who are hiding.

WAITER. You tell her. You've been a pitchman. You can talk.

ALL. Tell her. Tell her. Tell her.

COUNTESS. You're frightening me, my friends. Go on. I'm listening.

RAGPICKER. (*Rises, crosses to her.*) Countess, there was a time when old clothes were as good as new—in fact, they were better. Because when people wore clothes, they gave something to them. You may not believe it, but right this minute, the highest-priced shops in Paris are selling clothes that were thrown away thirty years ago. They're selling them for new. That's how good they were.

COUNTESS. Well?

RAGPICKER. Countess, there was a time when garbage was a pleasure. A garbage can was not what it is now. If it smelled a little strange, it was because it was a little confused—there was everything there—sardines, cologne, iodine, roses. An amateur might jump to a wrong conclusion. But to a professional—it was the smell of God's plenty.

COUNTESS. Well?

RAGPICKER. Countess, the world has changed.

COUNTESS. Nonsense. How could it change? The people are the same, I hope.

RAGPICKER. No, Countess. The people are not the same. The people are different. There's been an invasion. From another planet. An infiltration. The world is not beautiful any more. It's not happy.

COUNTESS. Not happy? Is that true? Why didn't you tell me this before?

RAGPICKER. Because you live in a dream, Countess. And we don't like to disturb you.

COUNTESS. But how could it have happened?

RAGPICKER. Countess, there was a time when you could walk around Paris, and all the people you met were just like yourself. A little cleaner, maybe, or dirtier, perhaps, or angry, or smiling—but you knew them. They were you. Well, Countess, twenty years ago, one day, on the street, I saw a face in the crowd. A

31

face, you might say, without a face. The eyes—empty. The expression—not human. Not a human face. It saw me staring, and when it looked back at me with its gelatine eyes, I shuddered. Because I knew that to make room for this one, one of us must have left the earth. A while after, I saw another. And another. And since then I've seen hundreds come in—yes—thousands.

COUNTESS. Describe them to me.

RAGPICKER. You've seen them yourself, Countess. Their clothes don't wrinkle. Their hats don't come off. When they talk, they don't look at you. They don't perspire.

COUNTESS. Do they have wives? Do they have children?

RAGPICKER. They buy the models out of shop windows, furs and all. They animate them by a secret process. Then they marry them. Naturally, they don't have children.

COUNTESS. What work do they do?

RAGPICKER. They don't do any work. Whenever they meet, they whisper, and then they pass each other thousand-franc notes. You see them standing on the corner by the Stock Exchange. You see them at auctions—in the back. They never raise a finger—they just stand there. In theatre lobbies, by the box office—they never go inside. They don't do anything, but wherever you see them, things are not the same. I remember well the time when a cabbage could sell itself just by being a cabbage. Nowadays it's no good being a cabbage—unless you have an agent and pay him a commission. Nothing is free any more to sell itself or give itself away. These days, Countess, every cabbage has its pimp.

COUNTESS. I can't believe that.

RAGPICKER. Countess, little by little, the pimps have taken over the world. They don't do anything, they don't make anything—they just stand there and take their cut. It makes a difference. Look at the shopkeepers. Do you ever see one smiling at a customer any more? Certainly not. Their smiles are strictly for the pimps. The butcher has to smile at the meat-pimp, the florist at the rose-pimp, the grocer at the fresh-fruit-and-vegetable pimp. It's all organized down to the slightest detail. A pimp for birdseed. A pimp for fishfood. That's why the cost of living keeps going up all the time. You buy a glass of beer—it costs twice as much as it used to. Why? 10% for the glass-pimp, 10% for the beer-pimp, 20% for the glass-of-beer-pimp—that's where our money goes. Personally, I prefer the old-fashioned type. Some of

32

those men at least were loved by the women they sold. But what feelings can a pimp arouse in a leg of lamb?—Pardon my language, Irma.

COUNTESS. It's all right. She doesn't understand.

RAGPICKER. So now you know, Countess, why the world is no longer happy. We are the last of the free people of the earth. You saw them looking us over today. Tomorrow, the street-singer will start paying the song-pimp, and the garbage-pimp will be after me. I tell you, Countess, we're finished. It's the end of free enterprise in this world! (DOORMAN *rises, crosses* R. *up of* RAG-PICKER.)

COUNTESS. Is this true, Roderick?

PIERRE. I'm afraid it's true.

COUNTESS. Did you know about this, Irma?

IRMA. All I know is the doorman says that faith is dead.

DOORMAN. I've stopped taking bets over the phone. (SERGEANT *rises, crosses* L. *of* DOORMAN.)

JUGGLER. The very air is different, Countess. You can't trust it any more. If I throw my torches up too high, they go out.

RAGPICKER. The sky-pimp puts them out.

FLOWER GIRL. My flowers don't last over-night, now. They wilt.

JUGGLER. Have you noticed the pigeons don't fly any more?

RAGPICKER. They can't afford to. They walk.

COUNTESS. They're a pack of fools and so are you! You should have told me at once! Why are you complaining instead of doing something about it? How can you bear to live in a world where there is unhappiness? Where a man is not his own master! Are you cowards? If these men are the cause of the trouble, all we have to do is to get rid of them.

PIERRE. How can we get rid of them? They're too strong.

COUNTESS. (*Smiling.*) The Sergeant will help us.

SERGEANT. Who? Me? (DEAF-MUTE *wigwags a short speech.*)

IRMA. There are a great many of them, Countess. The Deaf-Mute knows them all. They employed him once, years ago, because he was deaf. They fired him because he wasn't blind. (*Another flash of sign language.*) They're all connected like the parts of a machine.

COUNTESS. So much the better. We can drive the whole machine into a ditch.

SERGEANT. (*Crossing down to her.*) It's not that easy, Countess.

You never catch these birds napping. They change before your very eyes. I remember when I was in the detectives —— You catch a president, pfft! He turns into a trustee. You catch him as trustee, and pfft! he's not a trustee—he's an honorary vice-chairman. You catch a Senator dead to rights: wham! he becomes Minister of Justice. You get after the Minister of Justice—bango! he is Chief of Police. And there you are—no longer in the detectives.

PIERRE. He's right, Countess. They have all the power. And all the money. And they're greedy for more.

COUNTESS. They're greedy?

ALL. Yes, Countess.

COUNTESS. Ah, then, my friends, they're lost. If they're greedy, they're stupid. If they're greedy—(*Rises, moves between* RAG-PICKER *and* IRMA.) don't worry, I know exactly what to do. Pierre, by tonight you will be an honest man. And, Juggler, your torches will stay lit. And, Martial, your beer will flow freely again.—Come on, let's get to work. (DEAF-MUTE *crosses to her.*)

RAGPICKER. What are you going to do?

COUNTESS. Have you any kerosene in the house, Irma?

IRMA. Kerosene? Yes. I'll put some in a clean bottle for you.

COUNTESS. I want just a little. In a dirty bottle. With a little mud. And some mange-cure, if you have it. (*To* DEAF-MUTE.) Deaf-Mute! Take a letter. (IRMA *interprets in sign language.* IRMA *and* DEAF-MUTE *go into café. To* JUGGLER.) Juggler, go and find Madame Constance.

JUGGLER. Yes, Countess?

COUNTESS. Ask her to be at my house by two o'clock. I'll be waiting for her in my cellar. You may tell her we have to discuss the future of humanity. That's sure to bring her.

JUGGLER. Yes, Countess.

COUNTESS. And ask her to bring Mme. Josephine and Mlle. Gabrielle with her. Do you know how to get in to speak to Madame Constance? (*Crosses to him* D. R.) You knock twice and meow three times—do you know how to meow?

JUGGLER. I'm better at barking.

COUNTESS. Better practise meowing on the way. (JUGGLER *exits* R.) And, Singer, remind me to ask Madame Constance, I think she knows all the verses of your mazurka.

SINGER. Yes, Countess. (*Exit* STREET SINGER, R. IRMA *comes in*

34

with DEAF-MUTE. *She is shaking the oily concoction in a little perfume vial, which she now hands* COUNTESS.)

IRMA. Here it is, Countess.

COUNTESS. (*Crosses to* C.) Thank you, Irma. Ready, Deaf-Mute? (IRMA *interprets in sign language.* DEAF-MUTE *sits down table* C. *with* IRMA—*has pencil, envelope and a sheet of paper.*)

IRMA. (*Speaking for* DEAF-MUTE.) Ready.

COUNTESS. My dear Mr. —— What's his name? (IRMA *wigwags question to* DEAF-MUTE, *who answers in same manner. It is all done so deftly that it is as if* DEAF-MUTE *were actually speaking.*)

IRMA. They are all called Mr. President.

COUNTESS. " My dear Mr. President: I have personally verified the existence of a spontaneous outcrop of oil in the cellar of Number 21 Rue de Chaillot, which is at present occupied by a person of unstable mentality. (COUNTESS *grins knowingly. General amusement.*) This explains why, fortunately for us, the discovery has so long been kept secret. If you should wish to verify the existence of this outcrop for yourself—you may call at the above address at 3 P. M. today. I am herewith enclosing a sample so that you may judge the quality and consistency of the crude— Yours very truly. Roderick, can you sign the prospector's name?

PIERRE. You wish me to?

COUNTESS. One forgery wipes out the other. (PIERRE *crosses to* IRMA'S *chair, signs letter.* DEAF-MUTE *addresses envelope.*)

IRMA. (*Rising.*) Who is to deliver this?

COUNTESS. The Doorman, of course. On his bicycle. And as soon as you have delivered it, run over to the Prospector's office. Leave word that the President expects to see him at my house at three.

DOORMAN. Yes, Countess. (*Takes letter from* DEAF-MUTE.)

RAGPICKER. But this only takes care of two of them, Countess.

COUNTESS. Didn't I understand the Deaf-Mute to say they are all connected like the works of a machine?

IRMA. Yes.

COUNTESS. Then if one comes, the rest will follow. And we shall have them all.—My boa, please.

DOORMAN. The one that's stolen, Countess?

COUNTESS. Naturally. The one the Prospector stole.

DOORMAN. It hasn't turned up yet, Countess. But someone has left an ermine collar.

COUNTESS. Real ermine?

35

DOORMAN. Looks like it.

COUNTESS. Ermine and iris are made for each other. Let me see it.

DOORMAN. Yes, Countess. (*Exit* DOORMAN *into café*.)

COUNTESS. Roderick, you shall take me home. (*He rises.*) You still look pale. I have some old Chartreuse at home. I always take a glass each year. Last year I forgot. You shall have it.

PIERRE. Anything I can do to help you, Countess ——

COUNTESS. There is a great deal you can do. There are all the things that need to be done in a room that no man has been in for twenty years.—You can untwist the blind and let in a little sunshine for a change. There's the door on the wardrobe ——
You can take it off and deliver me once and for all from the old harpy that looks at me out of the mirror. You can let the mouse out of the trap. I'm tired of feeding it. (*To her friends.*) Each man to his post. See you later, my friends. (*General ad lib.* WAITER *into café*, FLOWER GIRL *goes out* R., PEDDLER, R., SINGER, R., DEAF-MUTE, L., SERGEANT, L. *All but* IRMA *and* RAGPICKER *leave. He moves to table* L., *she stands* R. C. DOORMAN *enters, puts ermine collar around her shoulders.*) Thanks very much. It's rabbit. (*Chime, one.*) Your arm, Valentine.

PIERRE. Valentine?

COUNTESS. Didn't you hear one o'clock strike? At one, all men become Valentine.

PIERRE. (*Offering his arm.*) Permit me.

COUNTESS. (*Starting off* R.) —Or Valentino. It's obviously far from the same. But they do have that much choice. (DOORMAN *hands her parasol.*) Thank you, my boy. (*She sweeps out majestically with* PIERRE R. RAGPICKER *crosses to* IRMA, *hands her a daisy, starts to speak, then shakes his head and leaves* L.)

IRMA. (*Clearing off table.*) I hate ugliness. I love beauty. I hate meanness. I adore kindness. It may not seem so grand to some to be a waitress in Paris. I love it. A waitress meets all sorts of people. She observes life. I hate to be alone. I love people.—But I have never said " I love you " to a man. Men try to make me say it. They put their arms around me—I pretend I don't see it. They pinch me—I pretend I don't feel it. They kiss me—I pretend I don't know it. They take me out in the evening, and make me drink—but I'm careful, I never say it. If they don't like it, they can leave me alone. Because when I say " I love you " to Him, He will know just by looking in my eyes that many have held me and pinched me and kissed me, but I have never said " I love you " to anyone in the world before. Never. No. (*Looking off in direction in which* PIERRE *has gone, she whispers softly:*) I love you.

WAITER. (*From within café.*) Irma!

IRMA. Coming. (*Exits.*)

CURTAIN

ACT II

SCENE: *The cellar of the* COUNTESS' *house. An ancient vault set deep in the ground, with walls of solid masonry, part brick and part great ashlars, mossy and sweating. In corners of cellar are piled casks, packing cases, bird-cages, and other odds and ends—the accumulation of centuries—the whole effect utterly fantastic. In* C. *of the vast underground room, some furniture has been arranged to give an impression of a sitting-room of the 1890's. There is a venerable bed piled with cushions that once were gay, three armchairs, a table with an oil lamp and a bowl of flowers, a packing-box marked "Fragile," a shaggy rug. It is 2 P. M. the same day.*

AT RISE: COUNTESS *is sitting over a bit of mending on bed.* IRMA *appears stage* L.

IRMA. Countess! The Sewer Man.

COUNTESS. You found him, Irma! Send him down.

SEWER MAN. (*Enters* L. *and bows.*) Countess!

COUNTESS. How do you do, Mr. Sewer Man. But why do you have your boots in your hand instead of on your feet?

SEWER MAN. Etiquette, Countess. Etiquette.

COUNTESS. How very American! I'm told that in America people apologize for their gloves when they shake hands. As if the human skin were nicer to touch than the skin of a sheep! And particularly when they have sweaty hands.

SEWER MAN. My feet never sweat, Countess.

COUNTESS. How very nice. But please don't stand on ceremony here. Put your boots on. Put them on.

SEWER MAN. (*Complying, sits chair* L.) Thanks, Countess.

COUNTESS. I'm sure you must have a very poor opinion of the upper world. The way people throw filth into your territory is absolutely scandalous!—I burn all my refuse, and I scatter the ashes. All I ever throw in the drain is flowers. Did you happen to see a lily float by this morning? Mine. But perhaps you didn't notice . . . ?

38

SEWER MAN. We notice a lot more down there, Countess, than you'd think. You'd be surprised at the things we notice. Lots of things come along that were obviously intended for us—little gifties, you might say—sometimes a brand new shaving brush— sometimes *The Brothers Karamazov* —— Thanks for the lily. (*Rising*.) A very sweet thought.

COUNTESS. Tomorrow you shall have this iris. But now I have two questions to ask you.

SEWER MAN. Yes, Countess?

COUNTESS. First,—and this has nothing to do with my problem— it's just something that has been troubling me—tell me—is it true that the sewer men of Paris have a king?

SEWER MAN. Oh, now, Countess, that's another of those fairy tales out of the Sunday Supplement. It seems to me these writers just can't keep their minds off the sewers! It fascinates them. They think of us moving around in our underground canals, like gondoliers in Venice, and it just sends them into a fever of romance. The things they say! They say we have a race of girls down there who are never permitted to see the light of day. It's completely fantastic! The girls naturally come out every Christmas and Easter. And orgies by candlelight with gondolas and guitars! With troops of rats that dance as they follow the piper. What nonsense! They're not allowed to dance. No—no—no. Of course we have no king. Down in the sewers you'll find nothing but good Republicans.

COUNTESS. And no queen—?

SEWER MAN. No. We may run a beauty contest down there once in a while. But no queen, what you call a queen. And as for the swimming races they talk about—possibly once in a while in the summer—in the dog days ——

COUNTESS. I believe you, I believe you. . . . Now, I must come to my second question, and I have very little time . . .

SEWER MAN. Yes, Countess.

COUNTESS. Do you remember that night I found you here in my cellar—looking very pale and strange—you were half dead, as a matter of fact, and I brought you some brandy?

SEWER MAN. Yes, Countess.

COUNTESS. That night you promised to tell me the secret of this room ——

SEWER MAN. The secret of the moving stone?

COUNTESS. I need it now.

SEWER MAN. Only the King of the Sewer Men knows this secret, Countess.

COUNTESS. I'm sure of that. I have three magic words that will open any door that words can open. I have tried them all—in various tones of voice. They don't work.—And it's a matter of life and death.

SEWER MAN. (*Crossing* R.) Look, Countess —— (*He locates a brick in masonry of the wall and pushes it once. A huge block of stone pivots and uncovers a trap from which a circular staircase winds into bowels of the earth. Lamp business.*)

COUNTESS. Heavens! Where do those stairs lead?

SEWER MAN. Nowhere.

COUNTESS. They must go somewhere.

SEWER MAN. They just go down.

COUNTESS. Let's go see.

SEWER MAN. No, Countess. Never again. That time you found me I had a pretty close shave. I kept going down and around and down and around for an hour, a year—I don't know. There's no end to it, Countess. And once you start, you can't stop—your head begins to turn—you're lost. No—once you're down there, there's no coming up.

COUNTESS. You came up.

SEWER MAN. I—am a special case. And I stopped in time ——

COUNTESS. Couldn't you have—shouted?

SEWER MAN. You could fire off a cannon.

COUNTESS. Who could have built such a thing?

SEWER MAN. Paris is old, you know—. Paris is very old ——

COUNTESS. You don't suppose, by any chance, there's oil down there?

SEWER MAN. There's only death down there.

COUNTESS. I should have preferred a little oil—or a vein of gold— or emeralds. You're quite sure there's nothing?

SEWER MAN. Not even rats.

COUNTESS. How do you lower this stone?

SEWER MAN. Simple. To open, you press here —— And to close it, you push there —— (*He presses brick. The stone descends.*) Now there's two in the world that knows it.

COUNTESS. (*To* C. *of bed.*) I won't remember long. Is it all right if I repeat my magic words while I press the stone?

SEWER MAN. It's bound to help. (IRMA *enters*.)

IRMA. (*Arranging chairs around packing-box*.) Madame Constance and Mademoiselle Gabrielle are here, Countess.

COUNTESS. Thank you very much, Mr. Sewer Man. Send them down, Irma.

SEWER MAN. (*Crossing* D. R. *to* D. L.) Like that story about the steam laundry that's supposed to be running day and night in my sewer. I can assure you, it's pure imagination—they never work nights. (*He exits* L., *while* CONSTANCE, *the Madwoman of Passy, and* GABRIELLE, *the Madwoman of Saint Sulpice, come on* L., *daintily.* CONSTANCE *is dressed all in white. She wears an enormous hat graced with ostrich plumes and a lavender veil.* GABRIELLE *is costumed with the affected simplicity of the 1880's with toque and muff. She is atrociously made up in a remorseless parody of blushing innocence, and she minces with macabre coyness.*)

CONSTANCE. Aurelia! Here we are! Don't tell us they've found your boa?

GABRIELLE. You don't mean Adolphe Bertaut has proposed at last! I knew he would.

COUNTESS. How are you, Constance? (*She shouts.*) How are you, Gabrielle? Thank you both so much for coming.

GABRIELLE. You needn't shout today, my dear. It's Wednesday. Wednesdays, I hear perfectly.

CONSTANCE. It's Thursday. (*To an imaginary dog who has stopped on landing* L.) Come along, Dickie. Come along. And stop barking. What a racket you're making! Come on, darling—we've come to see the longest boa and the handsomest man in Paris. Come on. (*Crossing to* R. *chair.*)

COUNTESS. Constance, it's not a question of my boa today. Nor of Adolphe. It's a question of the future of the human race.

CONSTANCE. You think it has a future?

COUNTESS. Don't make silly jokes. Sit down and listen to me. (CONSTANCE *and* GABRIELLE *sit.*) We have got to make a decision today, which may alter the fate of the world.

CONSTANCE. Couldn't we do it tomorrow? I want to wash my slippers. Now, Dickie, please!

COUNTESS. We haven't a moment to waste. Where is Josephine? Well, we'd better have our tea, and as soon as Josephine comes ——

41

GABRIELLE. Josephine is sitting on her bench by the palace waiting for President Wilson to come out. She says she's sorry, but she must see him today.

CONSTANCE. Dickie!

COUNTESS. What a pity she had to see him today! She has a first-class brain. (*She gets tea things from a side table, pours tea, and serves cake and honey.*)

CONSTANCE. Well, go ahead, dear. We're listening. (*To* DICKIE.) What is it, Dickie? You want to sit in Aunt Aurelia's lap? All right, darling. Go on. Jump, Dickie.

COUNTESS. Constance, we love you dearly, as you know. And we love Dickie, too. But this is too serious a matter. So let's stop being childish for once.

CONSTANCE. And what does that mean, if you please?

COUNTESS. It means Dickie. You know perfectly well that we love him and fuss over him just as if he were still alive. He's a sacred memory and we wouldn't hurt his feelings for the world. But please don't plump him in my lap when I'm settling the future of mankind. His basket is in the corner—he knows where it is, and he can just go and sit in it. (*Tea to* CONSTANCE.)

CONSTANCE. So you're against Dickie, too!

COUNTESS. I'm not in the least bit against Dickie. I adore Dickie. But you know as well as I that Dickie is only a convention with us. It's a beautiful convention. But that doesn't mean it has to bark all the time. Besides, it's you that spoil him. The time you went to visit your niece and left him with me, we got along marvellously together. When you're not there, he's a model dog—he doesn't bark, he doesn't tear things, he doesn't even eat. But with you around him, one really can't pay attention to anything else. I'm not going to take Dickie in my lap at a solemn moment like this —no, not for anything in the world—and that's that!

GABRIELLE. (*Very sweetly.*) Constance, dear, I don't mind taking him in my lap. He loves to sit in my lap, don't you, darling?

CONSTANCE. Kindly stop putting on angelic airs, Gabrielle. I know you very well. You're much too sweet to be sincere. There's plenty of times that I make believe that Dickie is here, when really I've left him home, and you cuddle and pet him just the same.

GABRIELLE. I adore animals.

CONSTANCE. If you adore animals, you shouldn't pet them when they're not there. It's a form of hypocrisy.

COUNTESS. Now, Constance, Gabrielle has as much right as you ——

CONSTANCE. Gabrielle has no right to do what she does. Do you know what she does? She invites people to come to tea with us. People whom we know nothing about, people—who exist only in her imagination.

COUNTESS. You think that's not an existence?

GABRIELLE. I don't invite them at all. They come by themselves. What can I do?

CONSTANCE. You might introduce us.

COUNTESS. If you think they're imaginary, what do you want to meet them for?

CONSTANCE. Of course they're imaginary. But who likes to have imaginary people staring at one? Especially strangers.

GABRIELLE. Oh, they're really very nice ——

CONSTANCE. Tell me one thing, Gabrielle.—Are they here now?

COUNTESS. Am I to be allowed to speak? Or is this going to be the same as the argument about inoculating Josephine's cat, when we didn't get to the subject at all?

CONSTANCE. Never! Never! Never! I'll never give my consent to that. (*To* DICKIE.) I'd never do a thing like that to you, Dickie sweet —— (*She begins to weep softly.*)

COUNTESS. Good Heavens! Now she's in tears. What an impossible creature! Everything will be spoiled because of her. All right, all right, Constance, stop crying. I'll take him in my lap.

CONSTANCE. (*Rises.*) No. He won't go now.—Oh, how can you be so cruel? Don't you suppose I know about Dickie? Don't you think I'd rather have him here alive and woolly and frisking around the way he used to? You have your Adolphe. Gabrielle has her birds. But I have only Dickie. Do you think I'd be so silly about him if it wasn't that it's only by pretending that he's here all the time that I get him to come sometimes, really? Next time I won't bring him! (*Sits.*)

COUNTESS. (*Rises, crossing* L.) Now let's not get excited over nothing at all! Come here, Dickie. Irma is going to take you for a walk. Irma! (*Rings bell.* IRMA *appears.*)

CONSTANCE. (*Crossing* L. *to below* COUNTESS.) No. He doesn't want to go. Besides, I didn't bring him today. So there! (*Back to her chair* R.)

COUNTESS. Irma, make sure the door is locked. (IRMA *nods and exits.*)

CONSTANCE. What do you mean? Why locked? Who's coming?

COUNTESS. (*Crosses to iron chair* C.) You'd know by now, if you'd let me get a word in. A horrible thing has happened.—This very morning, exactly at noon ——

CONSTANCE. Oh, how exciting!

COUNTESS. Be quiet!—this morning, exactly at noon, thanks to a young man, who drowned himself in the Seine—. Oh yes, while I think of it—do you know a mazurka called *La Belle Polonaise ?*

CONSTANCE. Yes, Aurelia.

COUNTESS. Could you sing it now, this very minute?

CONSTANCE. Yes, Aurelia.

COUNTESS. All of it?

CONSTANCE. Yes, Aurelia. But who's interrupting now, Aurelia?

COUNTESS. You're right. Well, this morning exactly at noon, I discovered a terrible plot. There is a group of men who want to destroy the whole city.

CONSTANCE. Is that all?

GABRIELLE. But I don't understand, Aurelia. Why should men want to destroy the city? It was they themselves who put it up.

COUNTESS. There are people in the world who want to destroy everything. They have the fever of destruction. Even when they pretend that they're building, it's only in order to destroy. When they put up a new building, they quietly knock down two old ones. They build cities in order to destroy the countryside.— They destroy space with telephones, and time with airplanes. Humanity is now dedicated to a task of universal demolition! I speak, of course, primarily of the male sex ——

GABRIELLE. (*Shocked.*) Oh ——!

CONSTANCE. Aurelia! Must you talk sex in front of Gabrielle?

COUNTESS. After all, there are two sexes.

CONSTANCE. Gabrielle is a virgin!

COUNTESS. Oh, she can't be that innocent. She keeps canaries.

GABRIELLE. I think you're being very cruel about men, Aurelia. Men are big and beautiful, and as loyal as dogs. I preferred not to marry, it's true. But I hear excellent reports of them from friends who have had an opportunity to observe them closely.

COUNTESS. My poor darling! You are still living in a dream. But one day, you will wake up, as I have, and then you will see what is happening in the world. The tide has turned. Men are changing back into beasts. I remember a time when the hungriest man was the one who took the longest to pick up his fork. The one who put on the broadest grin was the one who needed most to go to the bathroom. I remember, it was such fun to keep them grinning like that for hours. But now they no longer pretend. Just look at them—snuffling their soup like pigs, tearing their meat like tigers, crunching their lettuce like crocodiles!—A man doesn't take your hand nowadays—he gives you his paw.

CONSTANCE. Would that bother you so much if they changed into animals? Personally, I think it's a good idea.

GABRIELLE. Oh, I'd love to see them like that. They'd be sweet.

CONSTANCE. It might be the salvation of the human race.

COUNTESS. (Rises, crosses down R. To CONSTANCE.) You'd make a fine rabbit, wouldn't you?

CONSTANCE. I?

COUNTESS. Naturally. You don't think it's only the men who are changing? You'd change along with them. Husbands and wives together. We're all one race, you know.

CONSTANCE. You think so. And why would my husband have to be a rabbit if he were alive?

COUNTESS. Remember his front teeth? When he nibbled his celery?

CONSTANCE. I remember, I'm happy to say, absolutely nothing about him. All I remember is the time that Father Lacordaire tried to kiss me in the park.

COUNTESS. Yes, yes, of course.

CONSTANCE. And what does that mean, if you please? "Yes, yes, of course"?

COUNTESS. (By her.) Constance, just this once, look us in the eye and tell us truly—did that really happen or did you read about it in a book?

CONSTANCE. Now I'm being insulted!

COUNTESS. We promise faithfully that we'll believe it all over again after, won't we, Gabrielle? But just tell us the truth this once.

CONSTANCE. How dare you question my memories? Suppose I said your pearls were false!

COUNTESS. (Moves above iron chair.) They were.

CONSTANCE. I'm not asking what they were. I'm asking what they are. Are they false, or are they real?

COUNTESS. Everyone knows that when you wear pearls, little by little they become real.

CONSTANCE. And isn't it the same with memories?

COUNTESS. (*Sitting iron chair.*) Now, do not let us waste time. I must go on.

CONSTANCE. Furthermore, I think Gabrielle is perfectly right about men. There are still plenty of men who haven't changed a bit. There's an old senator who bows to Gabrielle every day when he passes her, in front of the palace. And he takes off his hat each time.

GABRIELLE. That's perfectly true, Aurelia. He's always pushing an empty baby carriage. And he always stops and bows.

COUNTESS. Don't be taken in, Gabrielle. It's all make-believe. I warn you, Gabrielle, don't let this senator with the empty baby carriage pull the wool over your eyes.

GABRIELLE. He's really the soul of courtesy. He seems very correct.

COUNTESS. Believe me, those are the worst ones. Gabrielle, beware! He'll make you put on black riding boots, while he dances the can-can around you, singing God knows what filth at the top of his voice. The very thought makes one's blood run cold!

GABRIELLE. You think that's what he has in mind?

COUNTESS. Of course. Men have lost all sense of decency. And besides, they're disgusting. Look at them in the evening, sitting at their tables in the cafés, working away in unison with their toothpicks, hour after hour, digging up roast beef, veal, onion ——

CONSTANCE. They don't harm anyone that way.

COUNTESS. Then why do you barricade your door, and make your friends meow before you let them come up?—Incidentally, we must make a charming sight, Gabrielle and I, yowling like tomcats on your doorstep.

CONSTANCE. There's no need whatever for you to yowl together. One would be quite enough.—And you know perfectly well why. It's because there are murderers. (*Rises, moves* R.)

COUNTESS. I don't quite see what prevents murderers from meowing like anyone else.—But why are there murderers?

CONSTANCE. Why? Because there are thieves!

COUNTESS. And why are there thieves? Why is there practically nothing but thieves?

CONSTANCE. Because they worship money. Because money is king.

COUNTESS. Ah—now we've come to it! Because we live in the reign of the Golden Calf. Did you realize that, Gabrielle? Men now publicly worship the Golden Calf!

GABRIELLE. (*Rises.*) How awful! Have the authorities been notified?

COUNTESS. The authorities do it themselves, Gabrielle.

GABRIELLE. Has anyone talked to the bishop?

COUNTESS. (*As* GABRIELLE *sits.*) Nowadays only money talks to the bishop. And so you see why I asked you to come here today. The world has gone out of its mind. Unless we do something, humanity is doomed! Have you any suggestions, Constance?

CONSTANCE. (*Sitting.*) I know what I always do in a case like this ——

COUNTESS. You write to the Prime Minister.

CONSTANCE. He always does what I tell him.

COUNTESS. Does he ever answer your letters?

CONSTANCE. He knows I prefer him not to. It might excite gossip. Besides, I don't always write. Sometimes I wire. The time I told him about the Archbishop's frigidaire, it was by wire. And they sent him a new one the very next day.

COUNTESS. There was probably a commission in it for someone. What do you suggest, Gabrielle?

CONSTANCE. Now, how can she tell you until she's consulted her voices?

GABRIELLE. I'll go right home and consult them, if you want, and we could meet again after dinner.

COUNTESS. There's no time for that. Besides, in my opinion, your voices aren't real voices at all.

GABRIELLE. (*Rising, furious.*) How do you dare say a thing like that?

COUNTESS. Where do your voices come from? Still from your sewing-machine?

GABRIELLE. Not at all. They've passed into my hot water bottle. And it's much nicer that way. They don't chatter any more. They gurgle. But they haven't been a bit nice to me lately. Last night they kept telling me to let my canaries out: "Let them out. Let them out. Let them out."

COUNTESS. Did you?

GABRIELLE. (*Sits.*) I opened the cage—but they wouldn't go.

47

COUNTESS. I don't call that voices. Objects talk—everyone knows that. It's the principle of the phonograph. But to ask a hot water bottle for advice is silly. What does a hot water bottle know? No, my dear, all we have to consult here is our own judgment.

CONSTANCE. Well then, tell us what you've decided. Since you're asking for our opinion, you've doubtless made up your mind.

COUNTESS. Yes, I've thought the whole thing through. All I really needed to know was the source of infection.. Today I found it.

CONSTANCE. Where?

COUNTESS. You'll see. I've baited a trap. In just a few minutes, the rats will be here. Don't be alarmed. They're still human.

GABRIELLE. Heavens! What are you going to do with them?

COUNTESS. That's just the question —— Suppose I get all those wicked men here at once—in my cellar—have I the right to exterminate them?

GABRIELLE. To kill them?

CONSTANCE. That's not a question for us. Better ask Father Bridet.

COUNTESS. (*Rises, crosses* R.) I have. Oh, yes. One day, in confession, I told him frankly that I had a secret desire to destroy all wicked people. He said: "By all means, my child. And when you're ready to go into action, I'll lend you the jawbone of an ass."

CONSTANCE. That's just talk. You get him to put that in writing.

GABRIELLE. What's your scheme, Aurelia?

COUNTESS. (*Pacing up and down.*) That's a secret.

CONSTANCE. (*Rises.*) It's not so easy to kill them. Let's say you had a tank full of burning oil all ready for them. You couldn't get them to walk into it. There's nothing so stubborn as a man when you want him to do something.

COUNTESS. Leave that to me.

CONSTANCE. But if they're killed, they're bound to be missed, and then we'll be fined. They fine you for every little thing these days.

COUNTESS. They'll never be missed.

GABRIELLE. I wish Josephine were here. Her sister's husband was a lawyer. She knows all about those things.

COUNTESS. Do you ever miss a cold when it's gone? When the world feels well again, do you think it will regret its illness? No, it will stretch itself and smile—and that's all.

CONSTANCE. Just a moment. Gabrielle! Are they here? Yes or no?

COUNTESS. What's the matter with you now?

CONSTANCE. I'm simply asking Gabrielle if her friends are in the room or not. I have a right to know.

GABRIELLE. I'm not allowed to say.

CONSTANCE. I know very well they are. Otherwise you wouldn't be making faces.

COUNTESS. May I ask what difference it makes to you if her friends are in the room?

CONSTANCE. Just this: If they are here, I'm not going to say another word! I'm certainly not going to commit myself in a matter involving the death sentence in the presence of third parties, whether they exist or not. (*Sits.*)

GABRIELLE. That's not being very nice to my guests, Constance.

COUNTESS. (U. C.) Constance, you must be mad! Or are you so stupid as to think that just because we're alone here, there's nobody else in the room? Do you consider us so boring or so repulsive that of all the millions of beings, imaginary or otherwise, who are prowling about in space looking for a little company, there's not one who might possibly enjoy spending a moment with us? On the contrary, my dear—my house is full of guests, always. They know that here, at least, is one place in the universe where they can come when they're lonely and be sure of a welcome and a pleasant hour. And for my part, I'm delighted to have them.

GABRIELLE. Thank you, Aurelia.

CONSTANCE. You know perfectly well, Aurelia ——

COUNTESS. I know perfectly well that at this moment the whole universe is listening to us—and that every word we say echoes to the remotest star. To pretend otherwise is the sheerest hypocrisy. (*Sits iron chair.*)

CONSTANCE. (*Rising and crossing* L.) Then why do you insult me in front of everybody? I'm not mean. I'm shy. I feel funny about giving an opinion in front of such a crowd. Furthermore, if you think I'm so bad and stupid, why did you invite me in the first place?

COUNTESS. (*Rises.*) I'll tell you. And I'll tell you why, disagreeable and quarrelsome as you are, I always give you the biggest piece of cake and my best honey.—It's because when you come there's always someone with you—and I don't mean Dickie—I mean another Constance, who resembles you like a sister, only she's young and lovely, and she sits modestly to one side and smiles at me tenderly all the time you're bickering and quarrelling, and never says a word. That's the Constance to whom I give the cake that you gobble, and it's because of her that you're here, and it's her vote that I'm asking you to cast in this crucial moment. And not yours, which is of no importance whatever. (*Sits.*)

CONSTANCE. (*Up to bed for cloak.*) I'm leaving.

COUNTESS. Be so good as to sit down. I can't let her go yet.

CONSTANCE. (*Crossing toward exit* L.) No. This is too much. I'm taking her with me. (IRMA *enters.*)

IRMA. Countess. Madame Josephine.

COUNTESS. Thank God.

GABRIELLE. We're saved.

(JOSEPHINE, *the Madwoman of La Concorde, sweeps in majestically in a get-up somewhere between the regal and the priestly.*)

JOSEPHINE. My dear friends, today, once again, I waited and waited for President Wilson, but he didn't come out.

COUNTESS. You'll have to wait quite a while longer before he does. He's been dead since 1924.

JOSEPHINE. (*Crosses* R.) I have plenty of time.

COUNTESS. (*Crosses to her, followed by* COUNTESS *and* GABRIELLE.) In anyone else, Josephine, these extravagances would seem childish. But a person of your judgment doubtless has her reasons for wanting to talk to a man to whom no one would listen when he was alive. We have a legal problem for you.— Suppose you had all the world's criminals here in this room. And suppose you had a way of getting rid of them. Would you have the right to do it?

JOSEPHINE. Why not?

COUNTESS. Exactly my point.

GABRIELLE. But, Josephine, so many people . . .

JOSEPHINE. (CONSTANCE *sits iron chair* C. COUNTESS, *chair* R. GABRIELLE, *chair* L. *Crosses* R. *to* L.) De minimis non curat lex. The more there are, the more legal it is. It's impersonal. It's even military. It's the cardinal principle of battle—you get all your enemies in one place, and you kill them all together at one time. Because if you had to track them down one by one in their houses and offices, you'd get tired, and sooner or later, you'd stop. I believe your idea is very practical, Aurelia. I can't imagine why we never thought of it before.

50

GABRIELLE. Well, if you think it's all right ——

JOSEPHINE. By all means. Your criminals have had a fair trial, I suppose?

COUNTESS. Trial?

JOSEPHINE. Certainly. You can't possibly kill anybody without a trial. That's elementary. No man shall be deprived of his life, liberty or property without due process of law.

COUNTESS. They deprive us of ours.

JOSEPHINE. That's not the point. You're not accused of anything. Every accused—man, woman or child—has the right to defend himself at the bar of justice. Even animals. (CONSTANCE *business.*) Before the Deluge, you will recall, the Lord permitted Noah to speak in defence of his fellow mortals. He evidently stuttered. You know the result. On the other hand, Captain Dreyfus was not only innocent—he was defended by a marvellous orator. The result was precisely the same. So you see, in having a trial, you run no risk whatever.

COUNTESS. But if I give them the slightest cause for suspicion— I'll lose them.

JOSEPHINE. (*Crosses L. to R.*) There's a simple procedure prescribed in such cases. You can summon the defendants by calling them three times—mentally, if you like. If they don't appear, the court may designate an attorney who will represent them. This attorney can then argue their case to the court, *in absentia,* and a judgment can then be rendered, *in contumacio.*

COUNTESS. (*Rises.*) But I don't know any lawyers. And we have only ten minutes.

GABRIELLE. Hurry, Josephine, hurry!

JOSEPHINE. In case of emergency, it is permissible for the court to order the first passerby to act as attorney for the defence. A defence is like a baptism. It's absolutely indispensable, but you don't have to know anything to do it. Ask Irma to get you somebody. Anybody.

COUNTESS. (*Crosses to bell.*) The deaf-mute?

JOSEPHINE. Well—that's getting it down a bit fine. That might be questionable on appeal.

COUNTESS. (*Calls.*) Irma!—What about the police sergeant?

JOSEPHINE. He won't do. He's under oath to the state. (IRMA *appears.*)

COUNTESS. Who's up there, Irma?

IRMA. All our friends ——

COUNTESS. And the Ragpicker?

IRMA. Yes.

COUNTESS. Send down the Ragpicker.

CONSTANCE. Do you think it's wise to have all those millionaires represented by a ragpicker?

JOSEPHINE. It's a first-rate choice. All criminals are represented by their opposites. Murderers by someone who obviously wouldn't hurt a fly. Rapists by a member of the League for Decency. Experience shows it's the only way to get an acquittal.

COUNTESS. But we must not have an acquittal. It would mean the end of the world.

JOSEPHINE. Justice is justice, my dear. (RAGPICKER *comes in* L., *with an air of importance. Behind him appear the other* VAGABONDS.)

RAGPICKER. Greetings, Countess. Ladies, my most sincere compliments.

COUNTESS. Has Irma told you ——?

RAGPICKER. She said something about a trial.

COUNTESS. We're about to summon before the bar of Justice all the wicked people of the world. You have been appointed attorney for the defence.

RAGPICKER. Terribly flattered, I'm sure.

JOSEPHINE. Do you know the defendants well enough to undertake the case?

RAGPICKER. I know them to the bottom of their souls. I go through their garbage every day.

CONSTANCE. What do you find there?

RAGPICKER. Mostly flowers.

COUNTESS. Are you trying to prejudice the case?

RAGPICKER. Oh, no, Countess, no. Permit me to make a suggestion. Instead of speaking as attorney, suppose I speak directly as defendant. That way it will be more convincing, and I will be able to get into it more.

JOSEPHINE. Excellent idea. Motion granted.

COUNTESS. We don't want you to be too convincing ——

RAGPICKER. Impartial, Countess, impartial.

JOSEPHINE. Have you had time to prepare your case?

RAGPICKER. How rich am I?

JOSEPHINE. Millions.

COUNTESS. Billions.

RAGPICKER. How did I get them? Theft? Murder? Embezzlement?

COUNTESS. Most likely.

RAGPICKER. Do I have a wife? A mistress?

COUNTESS. Everything. (VAGABONDS *react.*)

RAGPICKER. All right. I'm ready.

GABRIELLE. Will you have some tea?

RAGPICKER. Is that good?

CONSTANCE. Very good for the voice. The Russians drink nothing but tea. And they talk like anything.

RAGPICKER. All right.—Tea.

JOSEPHINE. (*Moving up to bed* C.) Officers, you will conduct the prisoner to the bar. (*To* VAGABONDS.) Come in, come in. You may all take your places. The trial is public. (VAGABONDS *dispose themselves.* RAGPICKER *is led to box* D. R. *of bed, placed by* POLICE-MAN.) Your bell, if you please, Aurelia.

COUNTESS. My bell. But suppose I should need it to ring for Irma?

JOSEPHINE. Irma will sit here, next to me. If you need her, she can ring for herself. Prosecutor, take your place. (COUNTESS *sits iron chair down* L. *of bed.* JOSEPHINE *sits on bed and rings bell.* RAGPICKER *mounts box.* GABRIELLE *sits stool* D. L. CONSTANCE *sits chair* L. *of* COUNTESS. DEAF-MUTE *between them.*) The court is now in session. You may take the oath.

RAGPICKER. I swear to tell the truth, the whole truth, and nothing but the truth.

JOSEPHINE. Nonsense. You're not a witness. You're a lawyer.

RAGPICKER. All right. I swear to lie, conceal and distort everything, and slander everybody. So help me God. (JOSEPHINE *rings stridently.* VAGABONDS *laugh.*)

JOSEPHINE. Quiet! Begin.

RAGPICKER. May it please the honorable, august and elegant court ——

JOSEPHINE. Flattery will get you nowhere. That will do. The defense has been heard. Cross-examination.

COUNTESS. (*Rising.*) Mr. President ——

RAGPICKER. (*Bowing with dignity.*) Madame.

COUNTESS. Do you know with what you are charged?

RAGPICKER. I can't for the life of me imagine. My life is an open book. My ways are known to all. I am a pillar of the church and the sole support of the Opera. My hands are spotless.

53

COUNTESS. What an atrocious lie! Just look at them!

CONSTANCE. You don't have to insult the man. He's only lying to please you.

COUNTESS. Quiet! You still don't get the idea. (*To* RAGPICKER.) You are charged with the crime of worshipping money.

RAGPICKER. Worshipping money? Me?

JOSEPHINE. Do you plead guilty or not guilty? Which is it?

RAGPICKER. Why, your honor ——

COUNTESS. Yes or no?

RAGPICKER. Yes or no? No! I don't worship money. Why, it's just the other way around. Money worships me. It adores me. It won't let me alone.

WAITER. Listen to that.

RAGPICKER. It's damned embarrassing, I can tell you.

COUNTESS. Defendant, you will tell the Court how you came by your money. (*Sits.*)

RAGPICKER. Certainly. The first time money came to me, I was a mere boy, a little golden-haired child in the bosom of my dear family. It came to me in the guise of a gold brick which, in my innocence, I picked out of a garbage can one day while playing. I was horrified, as you can imagine. I immediately tried to get rid of it by swapping it for a little rundown one-track railroad which, to my consternation, at once sold itself for a hundred times its value. In a desperate effort to get rid of this money, I began to buy things. I bought the Northern Refineries, the Galeries Lafayette, and the Schneider-Creusot Munition Works. And now I'm stuck with them. Everyone knows that the poor are alone to blame for their poverty. It's only just that they should suffer the consequences. But how is it the fault of the rich if they're rich? It's a horrible fate—but I'm resigned to it. I don't ask for your sympathy, I don't ask for your pity—all I ask for is a little human understanding —— (*He begins to cry.*)

COUNTESS. Dry your tears. You're fooling nobody. If, as you say, you're ashamed of your money, why is it you hold on to it with such a death-grip?

RAGPICKER. Me?

PEDDLER. You never part with a franc.

JUGGLER. You wouldn't even give the poor Deaf-Mute a sou.

RAGPICKER. (*Getting off box.*) Me, hold on to money? What slander! What injustice! What a thing to say to me in the presence

54

of this honorable, august and elegant court!—It's just the other way, ladies and gentlemen. I spend all my time trying to spend my money. If I have tan shoes, I buy black ones. If I have a bicycle, I buy a motor car. If I have a wife, I buy ——

JOSEPHINE. (*Rings.*) Order!

RAGPICKER. I despatch a plane to Java for a bouquet of flowers. I send a steamer to Egypt for a basket of figs. I send a special representative to New York to fetch me an ice-cream cone. And if it's not just exactly right, back it goes. But no matter what I do, I can't get rid of my money. If I play a hundred-to-one shot, the horse comes in by twenty lengths. If I throw a diamond in the Seine, it turns up in the trout they serve me for lunch. Ten diamonds—ten trout. Well, now, do you suppose I can get rid of forty millions by giving a sou to a deaf-mute? Is it even worth the effort?

CONSTANCE. He's right.

RAGPICKER. Ah, you see, my dear?—At last, somebody who understands me! Somebody who is not only beautiful, but extraordinarily sensitive and intelligent.

COUNTESS. I object.

JOSEPHINE. Overruled.

RAGPICKER. I should be delighted to send you some flowers, Miss —directly I'm acquitted. What flowers do you prefer, may I ask?

CONSTANCE. Petunias.

RAGPICKER. You shall have a bale every morning for the next five years. Money means nothing to me.

CONSTANCE. And amaryllis.

RAGPICKER. I'll make a note of the name. (*In the best lyrical style of the pitchman.*) The little lady understands, ladies and gentlemen. The lady is no fool. If I gave the deaf-mute a franc, twenty francs, twenty million francs—I still wouldn't make a dent in the forty times a thousand million francs that I'm afflicted with! Right, little lady?

CONSTANCE. He's right!

RAGPICKER. Money sticks to me like a mustard plaster. Like on the Exchange. If *you* buy a stock, it goes down like a plummet, but if I buy a stock, it turns arounds and soars like an eagle. If I buy at thirty-three ——

PEDDLER. I know. It goes up to a thousand.

RAGPICKER. It goes to twenty thousand! That's how I bought my twelve chateaux, my twenty villas, my 234 farms. That's how I endow the Opera and keep my twelve ballerinas.

FLOWER GIRL. I hope every one of them deceives you every hour of the day.

RAGPICKER. How can they deceive me? Suppose they try to deceive me with the male chorus, the general director, the assistant electrician or the English horn—I own them all, body and soul. It would be like deceiving me with my big toe.

COUNTESS. Don't listen, Gabrielle.

GABRIELLE. Listen to what?

RAGPICKER. No, no, I am incapable of jealousy. I have all the women—or I can have them, which is the same thing. I get the thin ones with caviar—the fat ones with pearls ——

COUNTESS. (Rises.) So you think there are no women with morals?

RAGPICKER. I mix morals with mink—delicious combination. I drop pearls into protests. I adorn resistance with rubies —— My touch is jewelled; my smile a motor car. What woman can withstand me? I lift my little finger—do they fall? Like the leaves in autumn —like tin cans from a second-story window ——

CONSTANCE. This is going a little far, I must say.

COUNTESS. You see where money leads?

RAGPICKER. Yes, of course, because when you have no money, nobody trusts you, nobody believes you, nobody likes you. Because to have money is to be virtuous, honest, beautiful, and witty. And to be without is to be ugly and boring and stupid and useless.

COUNTESS. One last question. Suppose you find this oil you're looking for. What do you propose to do with it?

RAGPICKER. (Mounting box.) I propose to make war! (VAGABONDS ad lib. reaction.) I propose to conquer the world!

COUNTESS. You have heard the defense, such as it is. I demand a verdict of guilty.

RAGPICKER. What are you talking about? Guilty? I? I'll have you know I am never guilty!

JOSEPHINE. I order you to be quiet.

RAGPICKER. I am never quiet!

JOSEPHINE. Quiet, in the name of the law!

RAGPICKER. I am the law. When I speak, that is the law. When I present my backside, it is etiquette to smile and to apply the lips respectfully. It is more than etiquette—it is a national privilege, guaranteed by the Constitution.

JOSEPHINE. It's contempt of court. The trial is over.

COUNTESS. And the verdict?

ALL. Guilty!

JOSEPHINE. Guilty as charged!

COUNTESS. Then I have full authority to carry out the sentence?

ALL. Yes, Countess.

COUNTESS. Then I can do what I like with them?

ALL. Yes, Countess!

COUNTESS. I can exterminate them?

ALL. Absolutely!

JOSEPHINE. (*Rings bell and rises.*) Court adjourned!

COUNTESS. (*To* RAGPICKER.) Congratulations, Ragpicker. A marvellous defense. Absolutely impartial.

RAGPICKER. (*Off box, moves to her.*) Had I known a little before, I could have done better. I could have prepared a little speech, like the time I used to sell spot removers ——

JOSEPHINE. No need for that. You did very well, extempore. Your style is reminiscent of Clemenceau—you have a great future. Good-bye, Aurelia. I'll take our little Gabrielle home.

CONSTANCE. I'm going to walk along the river.

STREET SINGER. Countess—my mazurka. Remember? You promised ——

COUNTESS. Oh, yes —— Constance, wait a moment. (*To* SINGER.) Well? Begin.

SINGER. (*Sings with guitar.*)

> Do you hear, Mademoiselle,
> Those musicians of hell?

(*Music cue, " La Belle Mazur."*)

CONSTANCE. Why, of course, it's *La Belle Polonaise* —— (*She sings.*)

> From Poland to France
> Comes this marvellous dance,
> So gracious,
> Audacious—
> Will you foot it, perchance?

JOSEPHINE. (*Reappearing at head of stairs.*)

> Now my arm I entwine
> Round these contours divine,

57

JOSEPHINE.
> So pure, so impassioned,
> Which Cupid has fashioned ——

GABRIELLE. (*She sings a quartet with others. The four* MADWOMEN *dance a mazurka.*)

> Let's dance the mazurka, that devilish measure,
> 'Tis a joy that's reserved to the gods for their pleasure—
> > Let's gallop, let's hop,
> > With never a stop,
> Let our heads spin and turn
> As the dance-floor we spurn—
> There was never such pleasure, such pleasure as this!

(*Mazurka offstage with violin. Music cue No. 2. All exit dancing, save* IRMA *and the* COUNTESS.)

IRMA. It's time for your afternoon nap.

COUNTESS. Thank you, my dear. Did you ever see a trial end more happily in your life!

IRMA. Just lie down and close your eyes a moment.

COUNTESS. But suppose they come?

IRMA. I'll watch out for them. (COUNTESS *stretches out on bed and shuts her eyes.* IRMA *tiptoes out. In a moment,* PIERRE *comes down softly, feather boa in his hands. He stands over bed, looking tenderly down at the sleeping woman, then kneels beside her and takes her hand.*)

COUNTESS. (*Without opening her eyes.*) Is it you, Adolphe Bertaut?

PIERRE. It's only Pierre.

COUNTESS. Don't lie to me. Say that it's you.

PIERRE. Yes. It's I.

COUNTESS. Would it cost you so much to call me Aurelia?

PIERRE. It's I, Aurelia.

COUNTESS. Why did you leave me, Adolphe Bertaut? Was she so lovely, this Georgette of yours?

PIERRE. You are a thousand times lovelier.

COUNTESS. She was clever, then?

PIERRE. She was stupid.

COUNTESS. When you looked into her eyes, you saw a vision of heaven, perhaps?

PIERRE. I saw nothing.

COUNTESS. That's how men are. They love you because you are

58

beautiful and clever and soulful—and they leave you for someone who is plain and stupid and soulless. But why, Adolphe Bertaut? Why? Why?

PIERRE. Why, Aurelia?

COUNTESS. I know she wasn't rich. Because when I saw you that time in the market, and you snatched the only good melon from right under my nose, your cuffs, my poor friend, were badly frayed ——

PIERRE. Yes. She was poor.

COUNTESS. It was on the way home from *Denise* that I first took your arm. Because it was windy and it was late. I have never set foot in that street again. I go the other way round. It's not easy, in the winter, when there's ice. One is quite apt to fall. I often do.

PIERRE. Oh, my darling—forgive me.

COUNTESS. No, never. I will never forgive you.

PIERRE. All the same, I swear, Aurelia ——

COUNTESS. Don't swear. I know. You gave her the same flowers. You bought her the same chocolates. No, I will never forgive you as long as I live.

PIERRE. I have always loved you, Aurelia.

COUNTESS. " Loved? " Then are you dead, too, Adolphe Bertaut?

PIERRE. No. I. love you. I shall always love you, Aurelia.

COUNTESS. Yes. I know that. That much I've always known. I knew *that* the moment you went away, Adolphe, and I knew that nothing could ever change it —— But I did want to hear you say it!

PIERRE. Don't forget me, Aurelia.

COUNTESS. And now, farewell, Adolphe Bertaut. Farewell. Let go my hand, and give it to little Pierre. (PIERRE *kisses her hand, then lets go, and rises.* COUNTESS *opens her eyes.*) Pierre? Ah, it's you. Has he gone?

PIERRE. Yes, Countess.

COUNTESS. I didn't hear him go. Oh, he makes a quick exit, that one. (*She sees boa.*) Good heavens! Wherever did you find it?

PIERRE. In the wardrobe, Countess. When I took off the mirror.

COUNTESS. Was there a purple felt shopping bag with it?

PIERRE. Yes, Countess.

COUNTESS. And a little child's sewing box?

PIERRE. No, Countess,

59

COUNTESS. Oh, they're frightened now. They're trembling for their lives. You see what they're up to? They're quietly putting back all the things they have stolen. But, dear me, how stupid they are! The one thing I really miss is my little sewing box. They haven't put it back? You're quite sure?

PIERRE. What was it like?

COUNTESS. Green cardboard with gold braid all around it.

PIERRE. It's not there, Countess.

COUNTESS. The thimble was gilt. I swore I'd never use any other. Look at my poor fingers —

PIERRE. They've kept the thimble, too. (IRMA *runs in excitedly with a decanter of water and some glasses on tray.*)

IRMA. Here they come, Countess! You were right — It's a procession. The street is full of taxis and limousines!

COUNTESS. I will receive them alone — (*As* PIERRE *hesitates to leave her.*) Don't worry. I'll take care of myself. Put the boa around my neck. Let them see me wearing it. (PIERRE *goes out.*) Irma—did you stir the kerosene into the water?

IRMA. Yes, Countess.

COUNTESS. Don't forget that I'm supposed to be deaf. I want to hear what they're thinking.

IRMA. Yes, Countess.

COUNTESS. (*Putting finishing touches to her make-up.*) I don't have to be merciful—but, after all, I want to be just — (IRMA *exits. As soon as she is alone,* COUNTESS *presses brick, and trapdoor opens.*)

IRMA. (*Off stage.*) Yes, Mr. President. Come in, Mr. President. You're expected, Mr. President. (*Announces.*) The Presidents of the Boards of Directors. (*Music cue No. 3.* PRESIDENTS *come down, led by* THE PRESIDENT. *They all look alike, dressed alike,* PRESIDENT. *They all look alike, dressed alike, and all have long and all have long cigars. They walk in rhythm, like figures in a dream.*) The Countess is quite deaf, gentlemen. You'll have to shout. (*Music cue No. 4.*)

1ST PRESIDENT. I had a premonition, Madame, when I saw you this morning, that we should meet again.

2ND PRESIDENT. Louder. The old trot can't hear you.

1ST PRESIDENT. I have a letter here, Madame, in which —

3D PRESIDENT. (*Shouts.*) Louder, louder. Is it true that you've located —

1ST PRESIDENT. —Oil? (COUNTESS *nods with a smile and points down.* 1ST PRESIDENT *produces a legal paper and a fountain pen.*) Sign here.

COUNTESS. What is it? I haven't my glasses.

1ST PRESIDENT. Your contract.

COUNTESS. Thank you. (*She signs.*)

2D PRESIDENT. (*Normal voice.*) What is it?

3D PRESIDENT. Waiver of all rights. (*He hands it to* 2D PRESIDENT.)

1ST PRESIDENT. (*Handing it to* 2D PRESIDENT.) Witness. (2D PRESIDENT *witnesses it.* 1ST PRESIDENT *passes it on to the* 3D PRESIDENT.) Notarize. (*Paper is notarized.* 1ST PRESIDENT *turns to* COUNTESS *and shouts.*) Now, Madame—(*He produces a gold-brick wrapped in tissue paper.*) Just show us the well, and this package is yours.

COUNTESS. What is it?

1ST PRESIDENT. Pure gold. Twenty-four karat—for you.

COUNTESS. Thanks very much. (*She takes it.*) How heavy it is!

2D PRESIDENT. Going to give her that?

1ST PRESIDENT. Don't worry. We'll pick it up again on the way out. (*He shouts at* COUNTESS, *pointing at trap-door.*) Is that the way?

COUNTESS. That's the way. (2D PRESIDENT *tries to slip in first.* 1ST PRESIDENT *pulls him back.*)

1ST PRESIDENT. Just a minute, Mr. President. After me, if you don't mind. (*Music cue No. 5. But as he is about to descend,* COUNTESS *steps forward.*)

COUNTESS. Just one moment ——

1ST PRESIDENT. Yes?

COUNTESS. Did any of you gentlemen happen to bring along a little sewing box?

1ST PRESIDENT. Sewing box? (*He pulls back another impatient* PRESIDENT.)

COUNTESS. Or a little gold thimble?

2D PRESIDENT. Not me.

3D PRESIDENT. Not us.

COUNTESS. What a pity!

1ST PRESIDENT. Can we go down now?

COUNTESS. You may go down now. (*Music cue No. 6.*) Watch

your step! (*They hurry down eagerly. When they have quite disappeared,* IRMA *appears and announces next echelon.*)

IRMA. The Prospectors!

COUNTESS. What? Are there more than one?

IRMA. There's a whole delegation.

COUNTESS. Send them down.

IRMA. (*Holding tray.*) Come in, please. (*Music cue No. 7.* PROSPECTOR *comes in, following his nose.*)

PROSPECTOR. (*Sniffing air like a bloodhound.*) I smell something. Who's that?

IRMA. It's the Countess. She's very deaf. (*Music cue No. 8. To other* PROSPECTORS.)

PROSPECTOR. Good! (PROSPECTORS *also look alike. Same business as* PRESIDENTS. *Sharp clothes, Western hats and long noses. They crowd after* PROSPECTOR, *sniffing in unison.* PROSPECTOR *is especially talented. He casts about on the scent until it leads him to decanter. He pours himself a glass, drinks it off, and belches with much satisfaction. Others join him at once, and follow his example. They all belch in unison.*)

PROSPECTORS. Oil?

PROSPECTOR. Oil!

PROSPECTOR. Traces? Puddles?

COUNTESS. Pools. Gushers.

PROSPECTOR. (*He drinks.*) Sixty gravity crude: straight gasoline! (*To* COUNTESS.) How found? Blast? Drill?

COUNTESS. Finger.

PROSPECTOR. (*Whipping out a document.*) Sign here.

COUNTESS. What is it?

PROSPECTOR. Agreement for dividing the profits. (COUNTESS *signs.*)

2D PROSPECTOR. What is it?

PROSPECTOR. (*Pocketing paper.*) Application to enter a lunatic asylum. (*To* COUNTESS.) Down there?

COUNTESS. Down there. (*Music cue No. 9.* PROSPECTORS *go down, sniffing.*)

IRMA. (*Entering.*) The gentlemen of the press.

COUNTESS. The rest of the machine. Show them in, Irma.

IRMA. The Public Relations Counsellors! (*They enter. Same dream effect. Music cue No. 10.*) The Countess is very deaf. You'll have to shout.

1ST PRESS AGENT. You don't say.—Delighted to make the acquaintance of so charming and beautiful a lady —— (*Music cue No. 11.*)

2D PRESS AGENT. Louder. She can't hear you.

1ST PRESS AGENT. What a face!

2ND PRESS AGENT. (*Shouts.*) Madame, we are the press. We fix all values. We set all standards. Your entire future depends on us.

COUNTESS. How do you do?

1ST PRESS AGENT. What will we charge the old trull? The usual thirty?

2D PRESS AGENT. Forty.

3D PRESS AGENT. Sixty.

1ST PRESS AGENT. All right—75. (*He fills in a form and offers it to* COUNTESS.) Sign here, Countess. This contract really gives you a break.

COUNTESS. (*Taking paper and pen.*) There's the entrance.

1ST PRESS AGENT. Entrance to what?

COUNTESS. The oil well.

1ST PRESS AGENT. Oh, we don't need to see that, Madame.

COUNTESS. Don't need to see it?

1ST PRESS AGENT. No, no—we don't have to see it to write about it. We can imagine it.

COUNTESS. But if you don't see it—how can you be sure the oil is there?

1ST PRESS AGENT. If it's there, well and good. If it's not, by the time we get through, it will be. You underestimate the creative aspect of our profession, Madame. (*She shakes head, handing back papers.*) I warn you, if you insist on rubbing our noses in this oil, it will cost you ten per cent extra.

COUNTESS. It's worth it. (*She signs. They cross toward trap-door.*)

2D PRESS AGENT. You see, Madame, we of the press can refuse a lady nothing. (*Music cue No. 12.*)

3D PRESS AGENT. Especially such a lady.

1ST PRESS AGENT. (*Going down, gallantly.*) It's plain to see, Madame, that even fountains of oil have their nymphs.—I can use that somewhere. That's copy! (*Music cue No. 13. As he goes, 1ST PRESS AGENT steals gold brick. There is a high-pitched chatter off-stage, and IRMA comes in, trying hard to hold back THREE WOMEN, who pay no attention to her whatever. These WOMEN are tall, slender, and as soulless as if they were molded of wax. They*

63

march erect and abstracted like animated window models, but chattering incessantly.)

IRMA. (*Offstage.*) But ladies, please—you have no business here— you are not expected —— (*To* COUNTESS.) There are some strange ladies here!

COUNTESS. I think we might let them come in, please, Irma. (*Music cue No. 14.* IRMA *goes. The* WOMEN *come in, without taking the slightest interest in their surroundings. As they pass* COUNTESS.) Who are you?

1ST LADY. Madame, we are the most powerful pressure group in the world!

2D LADY. The ultimate dynamic.

3D LADY. The mainspring of all combinations.

1ST LADY. Nothing succeeds without our assistance. Is that the well, Madame?

COUNTESS. That is the well! (1ST WOMAN *starts down.*)

2D LADY. Put out your cigarettes, girls. We don't want any ex- plosion. Not with my brand new eyelashes. (*Music cue No. 15. They go down, still chattering.* COUNTESS *rushes to* R. *wall and presses stone.*)

COUNTESS. My gold brick! Why, they've stolen my gold brick! (*She moves towards trap. It is now closed. Music cue No. 16.*) Well—let them take their god with them. (IRMA *enters and sees with astonishment that the stage is empty of all but* COUNTESS. *Little by little, the scene is suffused with light, faint at first but increasing as if the very walls were glowing with quiet radiance of universal joy. Only around closed trap a shadow lingers.*)

IRMA. What's happened? Where have they gone?

COUNTESS. They've evaporated, Irma. They were wicked and wickedness evaporates. (PIERRE *enters. He is followed by the* VAGABONDS, *all of them. The new radiance of the world is now very perceptible. It glows from their faces. Music cue No. 17.*)

PIERRE. Oh, Countess ——!

WAITER. Countess, everything's changed. Now you can breathe again. Now you can see.

PIERRE. The air is pure, the sky is clear ——

IRMA. Life is beautiful again.

RAGPICKER. (*Rushes in.*) Countess—the pigeons! The pigeons are flying!

FLOWER GIRL. They don't have to walk any more?

RAGPICKER. They're flying! Countess! The air is like crystal. And young grass is sprouting on the pavements.

COUNTESS. Is it possible?

IRMA. (*Interpreting for* DEAF-MUTE.) Now you can throw your fireballs up as high as you please—they won't go out.

FLOWER GIRL. And everywhere shopkeepers are smiling ——

SERGEANT. And on the street, utter strangers are shaking hands, they don't know why, and offering each other almond bars —— (*Music cue No. 18.*)

WAITER. Countess, we thank you! (*The lights dim. An unearthly voice is heard.*)

1ST VOICE. (*Off R.*) Countess!

2D VOICE. (*Off L.*) Countess!

3D VOICE. (*Off U. R.*) Countess!

1ST VOICE. Countess, we thank you. We are the friends of people.

2D VOICE. We are the friends of animals.

3D VOICE. We are the friends of friendship.

1ST VOICE. You have freed us.

2D VOICE. From now on there will be no hungry cats.

3D VOICE. And we shall tell the Duchess her dog's right name.

1ST VOICE. Countess, we thank you. We are the friends of flowers.

2D VOICE. From now on every plant in Paris will be watered.

3D VOICE. And the sewers will be fragrant with jasmine. (DEAF-MUTE *joins* COUNTESS D. C. *and speaks. Music cue No. 19.*)

DEAF-MUTE. Sadness flies on the wings of the morning—and out of the heart of darkness comes the light —— (*Music cue No. 20. The* ADOLPHE BERTAUTS *appear up* R., *move to* COUNTESS C.)

1ST ADOLPHE BERTAUT. Countess, we thank you. We are the Adolphe Bertauts of the world. We are no longer timid. We are no longer weak. Henceforth, for your sake, we shall hold fast to what we love—we shall be handsome—and our cuffs shall be forever immaculate and new.—Countess, we bring you this melon and with it our hearts —— (*They all kneel.*) Will you do us the honor to be our wife?

COUNTESS. (*Cries out.*) Too late! Too late! Too late! Too late! (*They take up their melons sadly, and go away.* VOICES *of* VAGABONDS *fade up meanwhile, all except that of the* DEAF-MUTE, *who once again becomes speechless.*)

PIERRE. Too late, Countess?

IRMA. Too late for what?

COUNTESS. I say that it's too late for them. On the 24th of May, 1881, the most beautiful Easter in the memory of man, it was not too late. And the day they caught the trout and broiled it on the open fire by the brook at Villeneuve, it was not too late. And it was even not too late for them the day the Czar visited Paris with his imperial guard. But they did nothing and they said nothing, and now—you two will kiss each other this instant!

IRMA. But, Countess ——

COUNTESS. It's three hours since you've met each other, known each other, and loved each other. Kiss each other quickly. (PIERRE *moves.*) Look at him. He hesitates. His happiness frightens him. How like a man! Oh, Irma, kiss him, kiss him. If you let a single instant wedge itself between you and him—it will become a month, a year, a century. Make them kiss each other, all of you, before it is too late, for in a moment his hair will be white, and there will be another madwoman in Paris, and before that moment comes —— (PIERRE *takes* IRMA *in his arms.*) Bravo! Oh, if you'd only had the courage to do that thirty years ago—how different I would be today! Dear Deaf-Mute, be still—your words dazzle our eyes. And Irma is too busy to translate for you —— (*They kiss again.*) Well, there we are. And you see how simple it all was? Nothing is ever so wrong in this world that a sensible woman can't set it right in the course of an afternoon. Only, the next time, don't wait until things begin to look black. The minute you notice anything, tell me at once.

RAGPICKER. We will, Countess.

COUNTESS. (*Her tone becomes businesslike.*) Irma. My bones. My gizzard.

IRMA. I have them ready, Countess.

COUNTESS. Good. (*She puts bones into her basket and starts for stairs.*) Four o'clock. My poor cats must be starved. What a bore for them if humanity had to be saved every afternoon. They don't think much of it, as it is.

CURTAIN

PROPERTY LIST

Act I

Water and wine glasses—liquor
Newspaper
Cigar and matches
Violets—bunches
1 French banknote
Decanter and glass
Small basket
Dinner bell
3 scarves
Pocket mirror

Lipstick
Notebook and pencil
Glass of beer
Brass button
Parasol
Small bottle (with muddy liquid)
Pencil, envelope, sheet of paper
Ermine collar
Daisy
Juggler's implements

Act II

Mending materials
Bird cages and various accumulations of odds and ends
Boots (sewer man)
Tea things, cake, honey
Hand bell
Feather boa
Decanter of water and glasses

Several long cigars
Legal papers—several
Fountain pen
Gold brick
Cigarettes and matches
Melons
Chicken bones

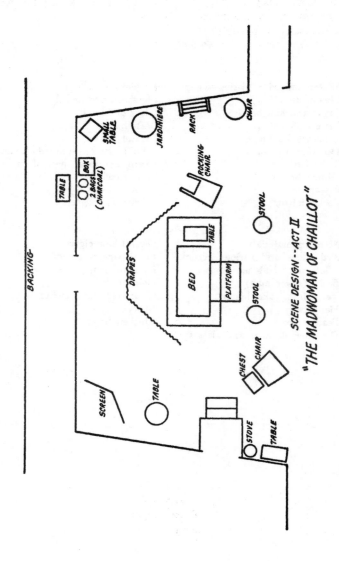

SCENE DESIGN -- ACT II
"THE MADWOMAN OF CHAILLOT"

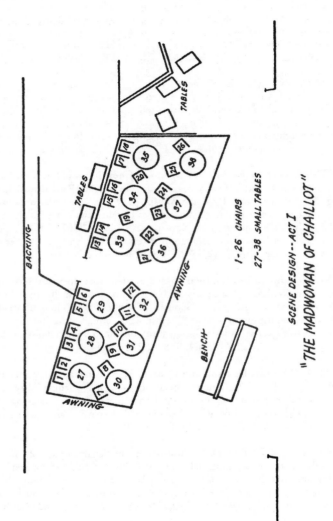

1 - 26 CHAIRS
27-38 SMALL TABLES

SCENE DESIGN -- ACT I
"THE MADWOMAN OF CHAILLOT"

NEW PLAYS

★ **THE PICTURE OF DORIAN GRAY by Roberto Aguirre-Sacasa, based on the novel by Oscar Wilde.** Preternaturally handsome Dorian Gray has his portrait painted by his college classmate Basil Hallwood. When their mutual friend Henry Wotton offers to include it in a show, Dorian makes a fateful wish—that his portrait should grow old instead of him—and strikes an unspeakable bargain with the devil. [5M, 2W] ISBN: 978-0-8222-2590-4

★ **THE LYONS by Nicky Silver.** As Ben Lyons lies dying, it becomes clear that he and his wife have been at war for many years, and his impending demise has brought no relief. When they're joined by their children all efforts at a sentimental goodbye to the dying patriarch are soon abandoned. "Hilariously frank, clear-sighted, compassionate and forgiving." –*NY Times.* "Mordant, dark and rich." –*Associated Press.* [3M, 3W] ISBN: 978-0-8222-2659-8

★ **STANDING ON CEREMONY by Mo Gaffney, Jordan Harrison, Moisés Kaufman, Neil LaBute, Wendy MacLeod, José Rivera, Paul Rudnick, and Doug Wright, conceived by Brian Shnipper.** Witty, warm and occasionally wacky, these plays are vows to the blessings of equality, the universal challenges of relationships and the often hilarious power of love. "CEREMONY puts a human face on a hot-button issue and delivers laughter and tears rather than propaganda." –*BackStage.* [3M, 3W] ISBN: 978-0-8222-2654-3

★ **ONE ARM by Moisés Kaufman, based on the short story and screenplay by Tennessee Williams.** Ollie joins the Navy and becomes the lightweight boxing champion of the Pacific Fleet. Soon after, he loses his arm in a car accident, and he turns to hustling to survive. "[A] fast, fierce, brutally beautiful stage adaptation." –*NY Magazine.* "A fascinatingly lurid, provocative and fatalistic piece of theater." –*Variety.* [7M, 1W] ISBN: 978-0-8222-2564-5

★ **AN ILIAD by Lisa Peterson and Denis O'Hare.** A modern-day retelling of Homer's classic. Poetry and humor, the ancient tale of the Trojan War and the modern world collide in this captivating theatrical experience. "Shocking, glorious, primal and deeply satisfying." –*Time Out NY.* "Explosive, altogether breathtaking." –*Chicago Sun-Times.* [1M] ISBN: 978-0-8222-2687-1

★ **THE COLUMNIST by David Auburn.** At the height of the Cold War, Joe Alsop is the nation's most influential journalist, beloved, feared and courted by the Washington world. But as the '60s dawn and America undergoes dizzying change, the intense political dramas Joe is embroiled in become deeply personal as well. "Intensely satisfying." –*Bloomberg News.* [5M, 2W] ISBN: 978-0-8222-2699-4

DRAMATISTS PLAY SERVICE, INC.
440 Park Avenue South, New York, NY 10016 212-683-8960 Fax 212-213-1539
postmaster@dramatists.com www.dramatists.com

NEW PLAYS

★ **BENGAL TIGER AT THE BAGHDAD ZOO by Rajiv Joseph.** The lives of two American Marines and an Iraqi translator are forever changed by an encounter with a quick-witted tiger who haunts the streets of war-torn Baghdad. "[A] boldly imagined, harrowing and surprisingly funny drama." –*NY Times*. "Tragic yet darkly comic and highly imaginative." –*CurtainUp*. [5M, 2W] ISBN: 978-0-8222-2565-2

★ **THE PITMEN PAINTERS by Lee Hall, inspired by a book by William Feaver.** Based on the triumphant true story, a group of British miners discover a new way to express themselves and unexpectedly become art-world sensations. "Excitingly ambiguous, in-the-moment theater." –*NY Times*. "Heartfelt, moving and deeply politicized." –*Chicago Tribune*. [5M, 2W] ISBN: 978-0-8222-2507-2

★ **RELATIVELY SPEAKING by Ethan Coen, Elaine May and Woody Allen.** In TALKING CURE, Ethan Coen uncovers the sort of insanity that can only come from family. Elaine May explores the hilarity of passing in GEORGE IS DEAD. In HONEYMOON MOTEL, Woody Allen invites you to the sort of wedding day you won't forget. "Firecracker funny." –*NY Times*. "A rollicking good time." –*New Yorker*. [8M, 7W] ISBN: 978-0-8222-2394-8

★ **SONS OF THE PROPHET by Stephen Karam.** If to live is to suffer, then Joseph Douaihy is more alive than most. With unexplained chronic pain and the fate of his reeling family on his shoulders, Joseph's health, sanity, and insurance premium are on the line. "Explosively funny." –*NY Times*. "At once deep, deft and beautifully made." –*New Yorker*. [5M, 3W] ISBN: 978-0-8222-2597-3

★ **THE MOUNTAINTOP by Katori Hall.** A gripping reimagination of events the night before the assassination of the civil rights leader Dr. Martin Luther King, Jr. "An ominous electricity crackles through the opening moments." –*NY Times*. "[A] thrilling, wild, provocative flight of magical realism." –*Associated Press*. "Crackles with theatricality and a humanity more moving than sainthood." –*NY Newsday*. [1M, 1W] ISBN: 978-0-8222-2603-1

★ **ALL NEW PEOPLE by Zach Braff.** Charlie is 35, heartbroken, and just wants some time away from the rest of the world. Long Beach Island seems to be the perfect escape until his solitude is interrupted by a motley parade of misfits who show up and change his plans. "Consistently and sometimes sensationally funny." –*NY Times*. "A morbidly funny play about the trendy new existential condition of being young, adorable, and miserable." –*Variety*. [2M, 2W] ISBN: 978-0-8222-2562-1

DRAMATISTS PLAY SERVICE, INC.
440 Park Avenue South, New York, NY 10016 212-683-8960 Fax 212-213-1539
postmaster@dramatists.com www.dramatists.com

NEW PLAYS

★ **CLYBOURNE PARK by Bruce Norris.** WINNER OF THE 2011 PULITZER PRIZE AND 2012 TONY AWARD. Act One takes place in 1959 as community leaders try to stop the sale of a home to a black family. Act Two is set in the same house in the present day as the now predominantly African-American neighborhood battles to hold its ground. "Vital, sharp-witted and ferociously smart." —*NY Times.* "A theatrical treasure…Indisputably, uproariously funny." —*Entertainment Weekly.* [4M, 3W] ISBN: 978-0-8222-2697-0

★ **WATER BY THE SPOONFUL by Quiara Alegría Hudes.** WINNER OF THE 2012 PULITZER PRIZE. A Puerto Rican veteran is surrounded by the North Philadelphia demons he tried to escape in the service. "This is a very funny, warm, and yes uplifting play." —*Hartford Courant.* "The play is a combination poem, prayer and app on how to cope in an age of uncertainty, speed and chaos." —*Variety.* [4M, 3W] ISBN: 978-0-8222-2716-8

★ **RED by John Logan.** WINNER OF THE 2010 TONY AWARD. Mark Rothko has just landed the biggest commission in the history of modern art. But when his young assistant, Ken, gains the confidence to challenge him, Rothko faces the agonizing possibility that his crowning achievement could also become his undoing. "Intense and exciting." —*NY Times.* "Smart, eloquent entertainment." —*New Yorker.* [2M] ISBN: 978-0-8222-2483-9

★ **VENUS IN FUR by David Ives.** Thomas, a beleaguered playwright/director, is desperate to find an actress to play Vanda, the female lead in his adaptation of the classic sadomasochistic tale *Venus in Fur.* "Ninety minutes of good, kinky fun." —*NY Times.* "A fast-paced journey into one man's entrapment by a clever, vengeful female." —*Associated Press.* [1M, 1W] ISBN: 978-0-8222-2603-1

★ **OTHER DESERT CITIES by Jon Robin Baitz.** Brooke returns home to Palm Springs after a six-year absence and announces that she is about to publish a memoir dredging up a pivotal and tragic event in the family's history—a wound they don't want reopened. "Leaves you feeling both moved and gratifyingly sated." —*NY Times.* "A genuine pleasure." —*NY Post.* [2M, 3W] ISBN: 978-0-8222-2605-5

★ **TRIBES by Nina Raine.** Billy was born deaf into a hearing family and adapts brilliantly to his family's unconventional ways, but it's not until he meets Sylvia, a young woman on the brink of deafness, that he finally understands what it means to be understood. "A smart, lively play." —*NY Times.* "[A] bright and boldly provocative drama." —*Associated Press.* [3M, 2W] ISBN: 978-0-8222-2751-9

DRAMATISTS PLAY SERVICE, INC.
440 Park Avenue South, New York, NY 10016 212-683-8960 Fax 212-213-1539
postmaster@dramatists.com   www.dramatists.com